MANAGING
COMMUNITY
DEVELOPMENT
IN THE
NEW FEDERALISM

Donald F. Kettl

MANAGING COMMUNITY DEVELOPMENT IN THE NEW FEDERALISM

Foreword by
James W. Fesler

PRAEGER

PRAEGER SPECIAL STUDIES • PRAEGER SCIENTIFIC

Library of Congress Cataloging in Publication Data

Kettl, Donald F
   Managing community development in the New Federalism.

   Bibliography: p.
   Includes index.
   1. Community development, Urban--Connecticut--Case
studies. 2. Federal-city relations--Connecticut--Case
studies. I. Title.
HN79.C83C64   353.9'746'008   79-23504

ISBN 0-03-053311-2

Published in 1980 by Praeger Publishers
CBS Educational and Professional Publishing
A Division of CBS, Inc.
521 Fifth Avenue, New York, New York 10017 U.S.A.

0123456789   038   987654321

Printed in the United States of America

To my mother and my father

FOREWORD by
James W. Fesler

In the evolution of American federalism two developments
have been particularly striking. One, dating from the 1930s, is
the bypassing of the states through direct federal grants to local
governments. The other, dating from 1966, is the enlargement of
recipient governments' freedom to determine how their federal
funds shall be used; this is the basic thrust of block grants and general revenue sharing. The Community Development Block Grant
Program, initiated in 1974, is one of a handful of federal programs
that incorporate both developments. Professor Kettl's penetrating
analysis of this program illuminates problems common to all
national-urban direct grant programs whose success rests largely
on local governments' performance in making choices and implementing them. The community development program's design, in
fact, makes this book both a study of federalism, and city government and politics.

The identifying feature of block grants in the federal system
is the delegation of discretionary authority to state and local governments to distribute their allocated federal funds among such
projects and programs as they choose within the field of a broadly
designated national purpose. This feature distinguishes block
grants from both categorical grants (for narrowly defined purposes)
and from general revenue-sharing grants (whose permitted purposes are legion). But to say that block grants fall between two extremes is to leave a wide range of possible placements. In the
dynamics of federalism any particular placement within that range
is likely to be unstable.

As time passes after initial enactment of a block grant,
Congress tends to adopt creeping-categorization amendments, par-
ticularizing the kinds of programs and projects that will qualify as
serving the national purpose. Block grants are swept together with
categorical and general revenue grants when Congress, in a suc-
cession of laws, imposes substantive and procedural conditions on
all federally aided state and local activities. As Dr. Kettl demonstrates, the breadth and ambiguities of block-grant legislative language invite the administering federal agency to interpret con-

gressional intent through guidelines, rules, and regulations. These may not only constrain recipient governments' discretion but also befuddle their officials when what was permissible yesterday is ruled impermissible today.

A block grant program does not exist in isolation from the complex intergovernmental environment. Within the policy field of such a program there are competing and complementary categorical aid programs and the alternative resource of general revenue-sharing funds. Local governments' proposed block-grant projects may encounter obstacles erected by federal and state laws, and agencies independent of the intergovernmental aid system (Dr. Kettl cites, among others, the federal mortgage insurance program, the state's Department of Environmental Protection, the Army Corps of Engineers, and federal and state agencies devoted to preservation of historic places). A block grant program neither monopolizes its policy field, nor is it static.

Few studies provide so intimate a view of city governments in action as does this one. Kettl tells us a great deal about the local communities studied, their interest groups' tactics and impact, and, most importantly, their governments' political and administrative capabilities. Though the focus is on exercise of options in use of community development funds and implementation of the choices made, what is revealed can inform judgments on a far wider front than that of this particular federal-aid program.

Dr. Kettl's spare prose and clarity of presentation make it all deceptively simple. Despite the fact that recounting the tales of four cities and eight community-development projects, juggling a multiplicity of variables, factoring out the several stages of program development and implementation, and identifying disparate and shared patterns of political and administrative behavior, are an undertaking of great complexity. The result is a model of how empirical investigation using the comparative case method can yield general propositions that have significance for national policy and that confirm or correct prevailing assumptions about political institutions and processes.

James W. Fesler

ACKNOWLEDGMENTS

A large number of public officials—in the U.S. Department of Housing and Urban Development and in the four Connecticut cities I studied—gave more generously of their time in my field research than any scholar could hope. They guided me through their files, dug out forgotten details, patiently answered my questions, and produced important insights. In return for their openness they were promised anonymity; quotations not otherwise attributed in this book come from my interviews with these officials. They have my deepest thanks.

I am indebted to many other persons for their guidance in helping me shape this work. James Fesler provided keen editorial judgment and sharp questions that always forced me to think out more clearly what I was trying to say. Douglas Yates both helped me to probe broader questions and generously provided a productive atmosphere in which to work. Raymond Duvall gave valuable advice in structuring the book's methodology. Garry Brewer, Stanley Greenberg, and Demetrios Caraley read earlier versions of this study and provided useful criticisms. The responsibility for any errors that remain in spite of their assistance is mine.

Fran Notaro, Gene Kaliszewski, and Sharon Wolford deciphered the signs and arrows on my drafts and carefully prepared my manuscript for publication. They all have my thanks. I am also grateful to Betsy Brown and the staff at Praeger for skillfully working the book into its final form.

Generous financial support from two organizations supported the research and writing of this book: the U.S. Department of Housing and Urban Development, and the Project '87 Joint Committee of the American Historical Association and the American Political Science Association.

Finally, I owe a special debt to my wife, Susan. More often than I can remember she patiently helped me through difficult times. That help deserves a lasting thanks here.

CONTENTS

LIST OF TABLES

MANAGING COMMUNITY DEVELOPMENT IN THE NEW FEDERALISM

1
THE DOUBLE DILEMMA OF FEDERAL GRANTS

FEDERAL GRANTS IN THE AMERICAN SYSTEM

Agents for Federal Policy

The founding fathers clearly saw the states as the strongest entities within the intergovernmental system they invented. The states would be the wellsprings of political power, and any power that the federal government enjoyed would flow from the support of the states. "Thus," Madison argued in Federalist Number 45, "each of the principal branches of the federal government will owe its existence more or less to the favor of the State governments." The Great Depression of the 1930s, however, stood the argument on its head. While large delegations of the unemployed marched on the Pennsylvania state legislature in 1933, the General Assembly spent two months arguing about a beer bill, a Sunday fishing bill, and a Sunday baseball bill.[1] The ineptitude of the states plus the urgent needs of their citizens prompted Franklin D. Roosevelt to seek a federal solution: the New Deal.

The alphabet of New Deal programs, from FERA to WPA, firmly established the federal government as the prime mover in intergovernmental policy. Furthermore, the New Deal set the federal conditional grant as the currency of intergovernmental exchange, with state and local governments employed as agents of national policy. The New Deal originated neither the trend toward centralization of government programs in Washington nor the use of federal grants. At the end of World War I, for example, scholars were commenting on the growing power of the national government.[2] Federal grants, furthermore, can be traced as far back as the 1785

1

federal land grants for state education. But the New Deal marked a quantum change in these arrangements: the grants represented much more significant amounts of money; they covered a far broader range of functions; and they sealed a national-level judgment of state and local government failure.

Thus, if the national government wanted to improve, say, highways or public assistance payments, it would fund the state or local governments to act as its administrative agents. And if state and local governments failed to meet their own obligations—for any reason, political, economic, or administrative—the federal government stood ready to reinforce their services with infusions of federal cash. It was, as Jane Perry Clark Carey explained in 1938, "the rise of a new federalism."[3]

The Failure of State and Local Governments

By the end of the nineteenth century, the states had already been indicted for failing to meet adequately their responsibilities.[4] Their boundaries, scholars charged, were illogical, too small for effective administrative regions and too large for responsive local government. Furthermore, their boundaries often split closely related economic regions and metropolitan areas. They often shirked their responsibilities, like meeting the problems of the Depression, and their failure quickened the drift of power toward the federal government.

The indictment of the cities, if possible, was even more harsh. The muckrakers, led by Lincoln Steffens and Upton Sinclair, probed the depths of bribery, vote fraud, and machine politics in the nation's big cities. At the conclusion of a contested primary election investigated by the U.S. Senate, Senator James A. Reed of Missouri noted that gaining entry to Philadelphia's voter registration list was one sure path to eternal life.[5] The fragmentation of local governments combined with municipal corruption prompted James Bruce to conclude in The American Commonwealth that "There is no denying that the government of cities is the one conspicuous failure of the United States."[6]

The Growth of Federal Grants

The tradition of state and local corruption and administrative incompetence—combined with their failure to meet the problems of the Depression—stimulated new federal efforts to solve domestic problems. It also created, at least to some degree, a sense of sanctimony and omnipotence at the federal level, a sense of virtue coupled with impatience about the limited abilities of state and local governments.

The result was a dramatic growth in federal grants to state and local governments. From the New Deal through Lyndon Johnson's Great Society and even Richard Nixon's New Federalism, the growth followed three consistent trends. First, federal grants to state and local governments accounted for a growing share of federal expenditures. Federal aid was only 8.8 percent of federal domestic expenditures in 1950. The amount grew to 16.5 percent by 1965 and 22.1 percent by 1979. (See Table 1.1.)

TABLE 1.1

Federal Aid to State and Local Governments

Year	Federal Aid as a Percent of:	
	Domestic Federal Outlays*	State-Local General Revenue from Own Sources
1950	8.8	—
1954	—	11.4
1955	12.1	—
1960	15.9	—
1964	—	17.3
1965	16.5	—
1970	21.1	21.4
1972	22.8	24.6
1974	23.3	25.8
1976	21.7	34.4
1978 (est.)	22.9	33.3
1979 (est.)	22.1	—

*Excluding outlays for national defense and international programs.

Source: U.S. Advisory Commission on Intergovernmental Relations, Significant Features of Fiscal Federalism, 1978–79 Edition (Washington, D.C.: U.S. Government Printing Office, 1979), pp. 77–78.

Second, federal grants became an increasingly important part of state and local government revenue. As Table 1.1 shows, only 11.4 percent of state and local general revenue from their own sources came from federal grants in 1954. By 1978, the share was exactly one-third.

Third, federal grants funded a wider range of functions, especially functions with increasing importance for the redistribution of national income. As late as 1932, 87.1 percent of federal grants paid for highway construction. By 1940, highway grants accounted for only 17.0 percent of the total, while social welfare grants rose to 54.9 percent. And by 1968, highway grants were only 23.1 percent of the total and social welfare grants had grown to 68.8 percent. [7]

Through the 1960s, nearly all of the grants were categorical—grants for narrowly defined objectives. In its study of the intergovernmental grant system, the U.S. Advisory Commission on Intergovernmental Relations identified four types of categorical grants: formula grants, where recipients were allocated funds according to factors contained in legislation or regulations; project grants, where potential recipients competed for funds through applications; formula-project grants, where potential recipients competed for funds allocated by a formula to their state; and reimbursement grants, where the federal government paid a specified share of state and local government program costs. [8]

As the intergovernmental grant system developed, there were occasional calls for reform. In 1955, the Kestnbaum Commission on Intergovernmental Relations contended that the narrow, highly specialized objectives of most federal grant programs brought high administrative costs and inadequate flexibility. "Elaborate supervision of grant objects," the commission said, "may sometimes thwart the best use of funds." [9] Allowing the states and cities to determine how to spend federal money within broad categories might simplify grant paperwork requirements and make the money more effective, the commission concluded.

Congress enacted two new programs in the next 15 years that followed the commission's recommendations and established a new kind of grant, the block grant: a broad-based grant entitling state and local governments to funds according to a formula and allowing recipients to spend the funds largely at their own discretion within broad functional categories. In 1966, the Partnership for Health Act consolidated 16 narrow-purpose categorical grant programs into a block grant for comprehensive public health services. Two years later, Title I of the Omnibus Crime Control and Safe Streets Act of 1968 established a broad-purpose grant to help the states and cities deal with the wave of urban riots and campus unrest.

Despite the emergence of the block grants, the categorical grants continued to dominate the intergovernmental system. The money was attractive to state and local officials no matter what package it arrived in. But by the late 1960s, the categorical grants— particularly the ambitious programs to save and rebuild the cities— were under siege.

Challenge to the System

Citizens, scholars, and politicians had generally conceded that the nation's attack through the categorical grant system on urban decay and poverty had failed. The Douglas Commission on urban problems argued in 1969 that the urban renewal program was beset with serious procedural problems and, furthermore, that the program had "failed to help the poor."[10] Model Cities, designed by Lyndon Johnson as a demonstration of the potential for restoring central-city neighborhoods, became according to one critic "the most unequivocal failure of all the 'Great Society' programs."[11] Despite the expenditure of billions of dollars over years of efforts, the cities had not been saved and, indeed, many neighborhoods appeared to be worse off.

The urban programs failed, the critics said, because of two problems that dogged many other federal grant programs to state and local governments. First, the administrative process for channeling money from the federal to the local governments was clogged by gross inefficiencies that blocked the effective implementation of programs. In a study of the grant system, the U.S. General Accounting Office found a host of problems: fragmentation of effort; lack of coordination among programs; competitive grantsmanship among local governments; and confusion, delays, and red tape.[12] The processing of urban renewal applications took an "unconscionable amount of time," according to the Douglas Commission—up to four years[13]—and the U.S. Department of Housing and Urban Development's (HUD) manual of regulations for the program filled four volumes. The Model Cities program plagued cities with "unrealistic and counterproductive planning requirements."[14] These problems spilled over to many of the other categorical programs whose very number—442 according to a count in 1975 by the U.S. Advisory Commission on Intergovernmental Relations[15]—inhibited coordination.

Second, the critics said that the grant system had produced a serious political imbalance: the national government subjugated state and local governments. Local government could use the grant funds only for narrow purposes outlined by the federal government, making "local fiscal management subject to the whims of outside funding."[16] Furthermore, the complexities of the federal grant programs led to an alliance among grant administrators at the national, state, and local levels—an alliance that helped them fend off attempts by elected officials to control the programs. The alliance "made coherent policy making and planning at the local level difficult and . . . diffused the locus of accountability."[17] The result was an alliance among administrators with narrow programmatic concerns and no ties of accountability to citizens—an alliance that, according to the critics, led to programs that either could not be implemented or did not serve local needs.

The criticisms were aimed predominantly at the project grants and were less applicable to the other varieties of categorical grant programs. The litany of charges against the project grants, however, became firmly fixed in the lore of the intergovernmental system and led to demands for change.

THE "NEW FEDERALISM"

Improving Governmental Performance

Richard Nixon responded in his 1971 State of the Union message with a call for a "New Federalism," a strategy to shift power in the federal system by changing the system of funding intergovernmental programs. Power had become too concentrated in Washington, he argued; it was time to "start power and resources flowing back from Washington to the states and communities."[18] Nixon pledged to "close the gap between promise and performance in American government"[19] by providing the states and localities "with more money and less interference."[20]

Nixon proposed a two-pronged attack. First, he set forth a restated version of the Heller-Pechman "general revenue sharing" plan[21] and advocated a $5 billion program of unrestricted grants to state and local governments. Second, he presented plans for consolidating a large number of federal categorical grant programs into six broad-purpose "special revenue sharing" programs—for urban development, rural development, transportation, education, job training, and law enforcement.

The special revenue-sharing proposals shared five distinctive characteristics. First, they were aimed at elected officials of general-purpose governments (state, county, city). Second, they consolidated a number of narrow-purpose categorical programs into broad-purpose grants. Third, they required no matching of funds from local sources as did many of the categorical programs. Fourth, entitlement of governments to the funds was automatic with the amount determined by a formula enacted by Congress. Finally, the block grants were designed to cut through red tape by giving state and local officials maximum discretion over the use of the funds within the broad purposes of the program.[22] The New Federalism demonstrated a preference for local over federal choice of priorities, for decision making by elected generalists over functional specialists at all levels.

General Revenue Sharing

Nixon's proposals for relatively unrestricted grants to all state and local governments found broad support. Congress passed his plan in 1972 and appropriated $30.2 billion for the first five years of the program, with local governments receiving two-thirds of the total. State officials could spend their money on anything but the required match for other federal grants. Local officials faced this plus another restriction: they could spend their money only within certain functional areas (including public safety, public transportation, health, recreation, social services, environmental protection, financial administration, and capital expenditures). In addition, none of the funds could be used for programs that discriminated against the poor.

Despite these restrictions, the general revenue-sharing program brought significant changes to intergovernmental fiscal relations. First, the grants went to all 50 states and to the approximately 38,000 general-purpose local governments. No previous federal grant program had the same reach into local finances. Second, state and local governments could use the money almost any way they wanted, in contrast with the categorical grant programs that earmarked the money for narrow functional areas. Finally, the program minimized paperwork requirements and stipulated only that recipients report how they used the money.

Special Revenue Sharing

The six special revenue-sharing programs faced a much more difficult time. Nixon designed them to continue the flow of federal money into specified functional areas and to minimize federal supervision of state and local activities. Allocations would be set by a formula to eliminate competition among eligible governments. Recipients would publish annual plans and outline their program objectives but review of the plans by federal agencies would be limited to commenting on, not approving, the proposals.

These features worried a wide range of interest groups and members of Congress. State and local governments might choose to ignore pressing national problems in spending their money if the federal government did not closely supervise the programs. They might, for example, ignore the needs of the poor and minorities and concentrate the money instead on the privileged. Furthermore, without federal supervision, mismanagement or perhaps even fraud might weaken the programs. The special revenue-sharing programs met a hostile reception in Congress—and died.

Two years later, the expiration of two federal manpower programs revived interest in the job training special revenue-sharing proposal. Congress again resisted Nixon administration arguments for vesting such significant discretion in state and local governments. Committee members agreed, however, on consolidating 16 federal categorical grant programs into broader categories and on decentralizing more program management responsibilities to state and local elected officials. The full Congress eventually concurred and passed the Comprehensive Employment and Training Act of 1973 (CETA), a block grant that shared many of the characteristics of the two earlier block grant programs.

The CETA program guaranteed annual entitlements to city and county "prime sponsors" (those with populations of at least 100,000 people); state governments could sponsor programs for the parts of the state not covered by other prime sponsors. Each sponsor prepared a plan to train the unemployed and underemployed. After review of the plans by the Department of Labor, each sponsor began the execution of its plan. Unlike earlier federal manpower programs, however, the state and local governments had primary responsibility for the administration of the CETA program.

In 1974, the urban development special revenue-sharing proposal also rose again but like CETA it was in a different form. Congress once more shied away from the special revenue-sharing approach, fearing that it delegated far too much responsibility to the cities. Instead, Congress followed the block grant model and enacted the Housing and Community Development Act of 1974. The act established Community Development Block Grants (CDBG), consolidating earlier categorical programs into a broad-based grant, guaranteeing eligible communities an annual entitlement, and allowing communities broad discretion in how to spend the money within a limited federal review. We will examine the details of the CDBG Program in more detail in Chapter 2.

Concerns about Performance

The CETA and CDBG programs joined the two earlier grant programs to establish the block grant as a significant new form of

federal aid. In 1966, there were no block grants and few general-
purpose grants.* Narrow-purpose grants like urban renewal and
highway grants accounted for nearly all of the federal aid money.
By 1976, general-purpose grants accounted for 12.1 percent of federal grants (due to the enactment of general revenue sharing) and
broad-purpose grants (composed mostly of block grants) grew to
10.4 percent. Narrow-purpose grants in 1976 were only 77.5 percent of all federal grants. (See Table 1.2.)

TABLE 1.2

Federal Aid by Category
(in percentages)

| Fiscal Year | Category of Grant | | |
	General-purpose	Broad-purpose	Narrow-purpose
1966	1.8	0	98.2
1968	1.6	0.3	98.1
1972	1.5	8.4	90.1
1976	12.1	10.4	77.5
1980 (est.)	10.6	11.3	78.1

Source: Data for 1966 and 1968, U.S. Advisory Commission
on Intergovernmental Relations, Improving Urban America: A Chal-
lenge to Federalism (Washington, D.C.: U.S. Government Printing
Office, September 1976), p. 87; subsequent years, U.S. Office of
Management and Budget, Special Analyses, Budget of the United
States Government, Fiscal Year 1980 (Washington, D.C.: U.S.
Government Printing Office, 1979), p. 230.

The new grant programs stirred up old concerns about state
and local performance. In addition to reviving old memories of
Boss Tweed and the Tammany Ring, critics also charged that local
governments were organizationally fragmented, administratively
inept, and politically unresponsive, particularly to minorities and
the poor.[23] And added to old criticisms about state ineptitude in
handling the Depression were new concerns that the states were

---

*These narrow-purpose grants included federal payments in
lieu of local property taxes and the federal payment to the District
of Columbia.

ignoring the needs of their cities. To vest responsibility for large sums of money with such irresponsible bodies of government, some critics charged, was both to abdicate federal responsibility and to invite fraud and waste. At the base of the critics' worries was a simple question: could the cities be trusted?

The New Federalism programs were also suspect because of three other economic concerns. First, the "perversity hypothesis," advanced by Alvin H. Hansen and Harvey S. Perloff in 1944, suggested that "the taxing, borrowing, and spending activities of the state and local governments collectively have typically run counter to an economically sound fiscal policy."[24] The New Federalism programs did not match exactly the conditions of the perversity hypothesis (the money spent was federal, not state and local) but the worries were the same: that the collective exercise of state and local discretion would produce results substantially different from national policy goals. Unresponsive local governments might ignore the needs of minority groups underrepresented among local political powers. State governments might ignore the needs of their cities.

Second, local performance in New Federalism programs with both an income redistribution and urban focus (particularly CETA and CDBG) were suspect because of traditional economic arguments about the proper governmental approach to redistribution. George F. Break argued that the proper role for unconditional grants is "to balance . . . basic fiscal deficiencies."[25] Programs that generate spillover benefits (that is, benefits to people outside a jurisdiction) or programs that attempt to concentrate benefits on a particular group require more narrow conditional grants, the economists argued. Thus, to the extent that some of the New Federalism programs pursued redistributive goals (and at least to some degree the CETA and CDBG programs did) and to the extent that the programs allowed cities substantial discretion in the use of the money (which in fact they did), the programs constituted an inefficient strategy for helping the poor.

Finally, New Federalism critics advanced an old principle of public finance: only when governments raise their money themselves can they be trusted to spend it well.[26] Relatively unconditional grants, the argument ran, weakened the ties of accountability that bound the public purse strings.

THE DOUBLE DILEMMA

The Conflict in Federalism

The conflict over the New Federalism philosophy traces its roots to the most enduring and unresolvable conflicts of the American republic: the relative power of the national vs. the state and local governments. Two different constitutions (the Articles of Confederation and the Constitution of the United States) and one civil war have scarcely settled the problem. The Kestnbaum Commission proposed one strategy in 1955:

> Leave to private initiative all the functions that citizens can perform privately; use the level of government closest to the community for all public functions it can handle; utilize cooperative intergovernmental arrangements where appropriate to attain economic performance and popular approval; reserve National action for individual participation where State and local governments are not fully adequate, and for continuing activity that only the National Government can undertake. [27]

This proposal, however, is more platitude than plan. Furthermore, behind the call for keeping governmental functions as close as practicable to the people lie five enduring intergovernmental principles which have traditionally served as a basis for intergovernmental policy:

1. Concentrate federal grants on the greatest national needs.
2. Maintain the integrity of state and local governments.
3. Assure adequate coordination among different federal grants.
4. Deliver the money to state and local governments with minimal administrative costs.
5. Manage grant programs effectively.

As we shall see, these principles are not mutually consistent.

Five Principles

Concentrate grants. All federal grants were born out of demands for federal attention to specific national problems. There are separate categorical grant programs to control automobile junkyards, to eliminate billboards, to experiment with highway pavement markings, to build secondary roads in rural areas, to construct interstate highways, and scores more just in the transportation area. Each categorical grant program focuses its funds on a narrow, concentrated problem in both a symbolic and material sign of federal attention to a problem.

Hand in hand with federal recognition of narrow policy goals is strict federal administrative control over grant funds to ensure that the money goes to those narrow areas. Without those controls state and local governments might not spend the money according to national policy. Recipients of Safe Streets block grants, for example, were criticized in the early 1970s for investing heavily in police technology instead of attacking crime. Concentrating federal money on narrow policy objectives implies close federal administrative supervision.

Maintain integrity. Among the many criticisms of the categorical grant system are the complaints that federal grants distort local planning. When state and local governments can apply their funds as the required match against a much larger amount of federal money, they might be inclined to alter their plans to take advantage of the "cheap" federal money. Furthermore, critics said, the vast number of grants dulled local initiative and creativity. With so many grants to choose from, Congressman Henry S. Reuss asked, "why search for new solutions to problems in fields not covered by the federal grants?"[28]

Furthermore, since administrative officials at all levels tended to dominate the grant system, elected officials tended to lose control over programs within their boundaries. Maintaining the integrity of state and local governments therefore implies greater control over the funds by state and local officials.

Assure coordination. With so many grant programs, some of the programs' objectives inevitably conflict. For years the Department of Agriculture paid farmers to drain wetlands and thereby increase production (often the production of crops already in surplus). At the same time, the Department of the Interior tried to convince the same farmers to convert their fields into wetlands to provide a resting spot for migrating wild fowl.[29] The federal government is simply not organized to coordinate the diverse federal programs affecting state and local governments. And even if there were a central coordinating agency, local conditions vary so greatly that program coordination at the federal level would be impossible. The alternative is to leave more discretion to state and local officials.

Minimize red tape. The tales of federal red tape in the urban renewal program became legendary—books of regulations measured by the yard, applications measured by the foot, and federal application reviews measured by the year. The Model Cities program produced still more volumes of plans, but the plans proved of little use in deciding which cities should get the funds. With most grants (particularly the project-based categorical grants) there were extensive regulations explaining what was and was not eligible for funding; long applications proposing what a city or state would do; lengthy

waiting periods while the federal administering agency decided
which proposals to fund; and administrative and accounting requirements if the proposal were approved. Minimizing these costs implies greater reliance on the administrative machinery of state and
local governments.

Manage programs effectively. The New Federalism proposals
to decentralize power within the federal system worried some observers of state and local government. A fundamental premise of
the New Federalism programs was that state and local governments
were capable of effectively managing the programs. However, the
long tradition of local ineptitude created the troubling suspicion that
the subnational governments lacked adequate administrative capacity.[30] Constitutional restrictions in many states limited the session
of state legislatures and fragmented state administrative structures.
State-imposed limits on local government taxing powers and rigid
civil service systems restricted local capacity. The result, according to a study by a federal commission, is that a fully competent approach to state and local government problems "is usually
beyond their existing management capacity."[31] (The supposition—
and a highly questionable one—is that the federal government pos-
sesses greater virtue and superior management capacity.) The demand for improved management, consequently, has often led to demands for greater control of grant policy by the federal government.

Political and Administrative Dilemmas

These five principles create a double dilemma. Half of the
dilemma is political: who shall decide how the money will be spent?
The other half is administrative: how effectively will the chosen
programs be implemented? Decentralizing power to state and local
governments seeks to maintain their integrity, to assure program
coordination, and to minimize red tape. But to decentralize power
runs the risk of diverting money from national policy goals and of
managing programs inefficiently.* On the other hand, centralizing
power within the federal government to protect national priorities
and to pursue better management runs the opposite risk: weakening
the integrity of state and local governments, creating program conflicts, and increasing red tape.

Obviously neither extreme can pursue all principles. Choices
between the extremes are possible but intermediate choices compro-

---

*This argument, again, is based on the questionable supposi-
tion of superior federal virtue and administrative capacity.

mise, at least to some extent, all five principles. The central problem of intergovernmental grant policy is thus to establish the desired levels of national control and local discretion.

The general revenue-sharing program would lie nearly at one extreme of an imaginary continuum between state/local discretion and federal control. The CETA and CDBG programs lie more toward the middle. They seek broad national policy goals within the framework of extensive local government discretion. They pursue coordination by allowing local governments to fund a wide range of projects. They trust that local governments will have the political capacity to select projects that attack their most important needs and the administrative capacity to implement the projects.

These programs establish a challenge to the cities. In the pages that follow, we will explore how four cities met the challenge in the CDBG program. Chapter 2 will examine in detail the background of the program and the methodology of this study. Chapters 3 and 4 will provide case studies of how the four cities handled the program's burdens. Chapter 5 will probe the political half of the dilemma: how the cities decided to spend their money. Chapter 6 will probe the administrative half: how effectively the cities implemented their projects. In Chapter 7 we will return to the principles we have outlined here to discuss the implications of the cities' performance for intergovernmental policy.

NOTES

1. W. Brooke Graves, American Intergovernmental Relations: Their Origins, Historical Development, and Current Status (New York: Charles Scribners' Sons, 1964), p. 806.

2. Walter Thompson, Federal Centralization (New York: Harcourt, Brace, 1923).

3. Jane Perry Clark Carey, The Rise of a New Federalism (New York: Columbia University Press, 1938).

4. See John W. Burgess, "The American Commonwealth," Political Science Quarterly 1 (March 1886): 9-35; and Simon N. Patten, "Decay of State and Local Government," Annals of the American Academy of Political and Social Science 1 (July 1890): 26-42.

5. Graves, American Intergovernmental Relations, p. 792.

6. James Bryce, The American Commonwealth, 3 vols. (London: Macmillan, 1888), vol. 2, p. 281.

7. U.S. Bureau of the Census, Historical Statistics of the United States, Colonial Times to 1970, Bicentennial Edition (Washington, D.C.: U.S. Government Printing Office, 1975), p. 1125.

8. U.S. Advisory Commission on Intergovernmental Relations, Categorical Grants: Their Role and Design (Washington, D.C.: U.S. Government Printing Office, May 1978), pp. 5-6.

9. U.S. Commission on Intergovernmental Relations (Kestnbaum Commission), A Report to the President for Transmittal to Congress (Washington, D.C.: U.S. Government Printing Office, June 1955), p. 132.

10. U.S. National Commission on Urban Problems, Building the American City (Washington, D.C.: U.S. Government Printing Office, 1968), pp. 165-67.

11. Christopher C. Demuth, "Deregulating the Cities," The Public Interest no. 44 (1976): 115.

12. U.S. General Accounting Office, Fundamental Changes Are Needed in Federal Assistance to State and Local Governments (August 19, 1975), p. 9. For other studies that reach similar conclusions, see Michael D. Reagan, The New Federalism (New York: Oxford University Press, 1972), pp. 86-88; and U.S. Executive Office of the President, Study Committee on Policy Management Assistance, Strengthening Public Management in the Intergovernmental System (Washington, D.C.: U.S. Government Printing Office, 1975), pp. 9-13.

13. National Commission on Urban Problems, Building the American City, p. 165.

14. Bernard J. Frieden and Marshall Kaplan, The Politics of Neglect: Urban Aid from Model Cities to Revenue Sharing (Cambridge, Mass.: MIT Press, 1975), p. 234.

15. U.S. Advisory Commission on Intergovernmental Relations, A Catalog of Federal Grant-In-Aid Programs to State and Local Governments: Grants Funded FY 1975 (Washington, D.C.: U.S. Government Printing Office, October 1977), p. 1.

16. Study Commission on Policy Management Assistance, Strengthening Public Management, p. 12.

17. Joseph D. Sneed, "Summary of Proceedings," in Restructuring the Federal System: Approaches to Accountability in Postcategorical Programs, ed. Joseph D. Sneed and Steven A. Waldhorn (New York: Crane, Russak, 1975), p. 2.

18. U.S. Office of the Federal Register, Weekly Compilation of Presidential Documents 7 (Monday, January 15, 1971), p. 92.

19. Ibid., p. 90.

20. Ibid., p. 93.

21. For an early formulation of the plan and the arguments supporting it, see Walter W. Heller, New Dimensions of Political Economy (New York: W. W. Norton, 1967).

22. U.S. Advisory Commission on Intergovernmental Relations, Special Revenue Sharing: An Analysis of the Administration's Grant Consolidation Proposals (Washington, D.C.: U.S. Government Printing Office, December 1971), pp. 9-10.

23. For a comprehensive examination of the criticisms, see Henry S. Reuss, Revenue-Sharing: Crutch or Catalyst for State and Local Governments? (New York: Praeger, 1970), pp. 37-70.

24. Alvin J. Hansen and Harvey S. Perloff, State and Local Finance in the National Economy (New York: W. W. Norton, 1944), p. 49.

25. George F. Break, Intergovernmental Fiscal Relations in the United States (Washington, D.C.: Brookings, 1967), p. 153.

26. Ibid., p. 139.

27. Kestnbaum Commission, A Report to the President, p. 6.

28. Reuss, Revenue-Sharing, p. 108.

29. Ibid.

30. See for example Douglas Yates, The Ungovernable City: The Politics of Urban Problems and Policy Making (Cambridge, Mass.: MIT Press, 1977).

31. Study Commission on Policy Management Assistance, Strengthening Public Management, p. vii.

2
BROADENING LOCAL RESPONSIBILITY

A NEW STRATEGY FOR URBAN AID

Steps toward Greater Local Discretion

By the mid-1960s, the federal government had developed a
large arsenal of weapons to attack urban poverty and blight. There
were urban renewal programs to clear old slums in preparation for
new development and Model Cities programs to deal with the complex economic and social problems within poor neighborhoods.
There were also federal programs to preserve open space, save
historic sites, develop water and sewer systems, construct neighborhood centers, and rehabilitate houses. But the arsenal was so
varied, local officials complained, that coordination of the weapons
was impossible. Control over the programs, furthermore, was
often out of their hands.

Two experimental programs between 1968 and 1971 tried to
resolve some of the problems. The Neighborhood Development
Program, begun in 1968, encouraged faster starts for urban renewal projects.* Three years later, the Planned Variations experiment in Model Cities gave some mayors more authority in running
local projects and expanded the program citywide. These experi-

---

*Throughout this book, I will use the term "program" to refer
to national policies, usually established by an act of Congress.
"Projects" will refer to local activities funded under these programs.

ments scarcely solved the problems with urban aid, but they did
mark the first steps toward Nixon's special revenue-sharing proposal for dramatic reform.

The urban development special revenue-sharing proposal met
hostile congressional criticism. Many members of Congress worried especially that the federal government would lose all control
over the money without a thorough advance review of local projects.
Congress held extensive hearings on the proposal but could not
muster the votes to pass it.

In an effort to pressure Congress into passing his community
development program, Nixon placed a freeze on federal spending
for the categorical development programs early in 1973. Nixon's
action, however, only delayed congressional action on the proposal
and worsened the president's already strained relations with Congress. In 1974, the pressures of impeachment politics left HUD
Secretary James Lynn with a relatively free hand in shaping a compromise version of the program from two conflicting bills: the
House version, which maintained many of the features of Nixon's
earlier program; and the Senate version, which insisted on greater
restrictions on the use of funds by local governments.

The bill that Gerald Ford signed in the first days of his presidency, the Housing and Community Development Act of 1974, was an
uneasy compromise between the two versions.[1] It was also a compromise between the categorical and special revenue-sharing strategies of aiding local governments: it greatly increased local political
and administrative discretion over the money yet maintained a measure of federal control.[2]

Provisions of the Program

The Housing and Community Development Act of 1974 established a new system for providing housing assistance to lower-
income families and extended the Department of Housing and Urban
Development's program for comprehensive local planning. The
most important feature of the act, however, was the establishment
in Title I of a $2.5 billion Community Development Block Grant
(CDBG) program.

The CDBG program consolidated seven of HUD's previous
categorical programs* into a single block grant program. The

---

*Urban renewal, Model Cities, water and sewer facilities,
open space, neighborhood facilities, rehabilitation loans, and public facilities loans.

program automatically entitled metropolitan cities (cities with a population of more than 50,000) and urban counties (counties with a population of more than 200,000) to an annual grant based on a "need" formula. The formula counted population, the overcrowding of a community's housing stock, and the extent of poverty (counted twice). Communities which had received a level of funding under the categorical programs higher than their entitlements were "held harmless": they would continue to receive the higher amount for the first three years of the program, and over the following three years would be phased down to the formula amount. The program also provided HUD with discretionary funds for nonmetropolitan communities, for the states, and for communities with urgent needs or innovative projects. None of the money needed to be matched.

To obtain funds, the program required the communities to:

- submit an annual application and a three-year community development plan;
- give "maximum feasible priority" to programs assisting low- and moderate-income families, or aid in the prevention of slums and blight, or meet urgent community development needs;
- develop a housing assistance plan which assessed the community housing needs and explained how the community proposed to meet those needs;
- give citizens adequate opportunity to participate in developing the plan and hold two public hearings to discuss the plan; and
- certify that it will comply with general federal grant requirements, including A-95 review procedures,* nondiscrimination, environmental protection, relocation, labor standards, and financial management, among others.

The program provided funds for three general goals: the elimination of slums and blight, the needs of low- and moderate-income families, and urgent local community development needs. Cities could spend their money on two general types of projects. Hardware projects were the core of the program, assisting cities with: rehabilitation of dilapidated housing; construction of neighborhood improvements such as parks and street lights; housing code enforcement; projects to remove architectural barriers to the handicapped; and other similar projects to develop "viable urban com-

---

*The Office of Management and Budget's Circular A-95 requires most grant applications to be submitted to state and regional clearinghouses for their review.

munities."[3] Communities could also use a portion of their entitlements to fund software projects—projects designed to improve

> the community's public services and facilities, includ-
> ing those concerned with the employment, economic
> development, crime prevention, child care, health,
> drug abuse, education, welfare, or recreation needs
> [of its citizens].[4]

The act gave HUD 75 days to review the applications and required HUD to approve applications unless:

■ the community's description of its housing and community
development needs and objectives was plainly inconsistent with generally available facts and data;
■ the community's proposed activities were plainly inappropriate to meet the needs and objectives; or
■ the community proposed ineligible activities or did not
otherwise comply with applicable provisions of the law.

Because the CDBG program was the result of a difficult compromise, the act set forth a large number of goals, some of which
were inconsistent. The most important objectives, however, were
procedural and substantive.[5]

Procedural. The CDBG program sought to simplify the application process for federal assistance and to reduce red tape. By
establishing a community's need by formula, the program attempted
to reduce the role of competitive grantsmanship. By granting communities broader discretion over the use of the funds, the program
attempted to reduce federal interference in local affairs. Most importantly, by emphasizing the relationship between local elected
officials and their constituents, the program sought to increase
local officials' accountability for results.

Substantive. The act defined the program's principal substantive objective as the development of "viable urban communities"
and spoke of the need to address the housing, living conditions, and
public service needs of lower-income families. The act also contained several other objectives, including more rational land utili-
zation and "spatial deconcentration" of housing for the poor. In
practice, however, not all of these objectives were consistent. Improvement of housing in a low-income neighborhood, for example,
may serve only to increase the "spatial concentration" of the poor.
The compromise between the House and Senate versions of the legislation left a complicated list of eligible activities and an uncertain
group of substantive goals.

NEW ROLES FOR INTERGOVERNMENTAL PLAYERS

The Path from Federal Control

The change in federal assistance for community development from competitive categorical grants to block grants changed HUD's role in intergovernmental relations from a predominantly <u>redistributive</u> role to a fundamentally <u>regulative</u> role. In the categorical programs, HUD pursued national policy goals by controlling who received funds for what. As local communities competed for a limited supply of funds, HUD conducted a thorough review of applications for assistance to insure that local communities had complied with proper federal procedures and then selected local programs that best met federal substantive goals. In carrying out the program, HUD officials often worked closely with their local counterparts.

It was precisely this extensive system of precontrols and federal intrusion into local government that sparked the New Federalism. Congress responded with the CDBG program, which sought the achievement of national policy goals through local action within a framework of general federal controls. The act gave HUD authority to conduct only a minimal review of applications to insure that applicants had met the basic procedural requirements for funding. According to the act, HUD's regulative role was to emerge in strong postcontrols through monitoring of local performance. Local officials carried the predominant burden for program performance. (See Table 2.1 for a summary of the differences between the two roles.)

HUD pursued its new role in a series of symbolic and substantive actions. First, in sharp contrast with the earlier categorical programs and their voluminous handbooks, HUD issued no book of rules. Instead, the rules HUD published in the <u>Federal Register</u> elaborated little on the wording of the legislation. To provide clarification of the regulations when questions arose, HUD Assistant Secretary for Community Planning and Development David O. Meeker, Jr., formed a "Critical Issues Group" from key members of his staff. The group reviewed questions of interpretation and provided answers to the field in what quickly became known as "Meeker Memos."

Second, aside from determining that an application did not contain "plainly inconsistent" objectives, "plainly inappropriate" projects, or ineligible projects, HUD permitted communities to sign "assurances" certifying that they had met the act's remaining requirements. Although HUD reserved the right to "consider substantial evidence that challenges the certifications," Meeker reminded the agency's field personnel that the certifications system "was deliberately established by Congress to place responsibility on the local governments rather than the Federal Government."[6] In a series of introductory sessions for local officials, HUD staff members continually stressed: "This is your program. We are not going to second-guess you, nor look beyond your certifications and if we get any citizen complaints about your performance, we will simply refer them to you."[7]

TABLE 2.1

Change in Intergovernmental Roles

	Categorical Grants	Block Grants
Role	Redistributive	Regulative
Method of distributing funds	Competition	Formula
Predominant form of control	Procedural and substantive	Procedural
Time of control	Precontrols	Postcontrols
Involvement of federal officials with local officials	Direct	Indirect

In addition to certification of compliance with the provisions of the Housing and Community Development Act, the assurances by local communities covered compliance with six other federal laws, two executive orders, two federal management circulars, and one Office of Management and Budget circular.* Among other things, the certifications dealt with financial management; civil rights and equal opportunity; relocation of persons displaced through CDBG projects; the Hatch Act; flood hazards; labor wage standards; and environmental reviews.

Third, HUD would monitor local performance at the end of the local "program years."† After a concentrated period of application

---

*These numbers are for the first year of the program. HUD made minor changes in subsequent years.

†The standard local "program year" began with HUD's approval of a community's application and ended 12 months later. The act, however, gave local communities the right to change the length of the

review, the field staff would spend the rest of the year visiting local communities and insuring that their activities met the program's requirements.

Criticism of HUD's Performance

The regulations left many questions unanswered, and the imaginations of local officials stretched interpretations of the regulations broadly. The act clearly made the acquisition of land and construction of recreational facilities eligible. But what about the acquisition of beach cleaning equipment to improve an oceanside park or the construction of tennis courts in a relatively affluent neighborhood? (HUD ruled the first ineligible, the second eligible.) HUD had intentionally left the regulations vague to avoid limiting local discretion. Local officials responded by probing and stretching the boundaries of interpretation.

Differences in interpretation among HUD's area offices produced inconsistency in the agency's review of local applications. [8] Communities found that they could search for an agreeable opinion for a planned project, either bypassing the area office and going to the regional or central office or showing that another community under the jurisdiction of a different area office had received a different ruling. "If you don't like what one office is doing, you can go to another—you can get an opinion from just about anyone" in HUD, one agency official explained. Some HUD area offices objected to any software programs at all, some maintained the 20 percent limit suggested but not mandated by the congressional conference committee on the act, [9] and others set no limit at all. [10] And some area offices approved applications with ineligible activities. [11] Although many of the variations in interpreting the regulations came on the margin, "that's where crucial decisions come," one HUD official explained.

The requirement that local governments give "maximum feasible priority" to the needs of low- and moderate-income families proved particularly troublesome. A survey by the General Accounting Office of 20 federal and local officials discovered that half of the

---

"year" by as much as a month in either direction. Many communities took advantage of this option to match the CDBG year to local budgetary cycles. Consequently, the beginning, end, and sometimes even the length of the CDBG "year" varied widely among local communities.

officials thought the term was undefinable or had little meaning; the other half responded with a wide variety of interpretations. [12]

HUD's monitoring activities also proved weak. One HUD area office staff member admitted, "I don't think we really know what is going on in the communities." The reasons were two: first, HUD did not have adequate manpower to examine local performance thoroughly; and second, the evaluation methodology HUD used was designed not to intrude deeply into local affairs. As a consequence, HUD had little information on the performance of local communities in the program.

Manpower. The two-phase administrative process envisioned by HUD officials early in the program—concentrated periods of application reviews followed by extended periods of monitoring—never had a chance to develop. HUD staff found that the application review period for entitlement communities stretched out longer than expected and the applications from communities seeking discretionary funds produced an enormous workload. HUD reviewed the applications of approximately 1,400 entitlement communities annually. In the first year of the program, however, HUD also funded more than 2,000 discretionary recipients and the number grew to 5,500 in the second year of the program. Reviewing the application of a small town which hoped to receive a $50,000 discretionary grant required nearly as much time as reviewing the application of an entitlement community for $5 million. The demands of both kinds of application reviews on HUD's manpower left little time for monitoring.

Methodology. HUD established two kinds of monitoring: performance monitoring, to examine how well local communities met the objectives and requirements of the act; and compliance monitoring, to examine how well local communities met the requirements of the other federal laws applicable to the act and listed in the assurances. The agency's central office staff stressed that monitoring visits by field personnel should intrude minimally into local affairs. In one training session, for example, a central office official explained the procedure by using an analogy of evaluating a bridge built across a river. It doesn't matter, he said, if it is a pretty bridge or even if it reaches across to the other side. What is important is whether in building the bridge the community discriminated (say, by building it principally for the use of high-income families), whether the community paid the laborers according to proper wage standards, whether the community assessed the environmental impact of the bridge, or whether the community allowed for citizen input into the planning for the bridge. In short, on-site monitoring visits, both for procedure and compliance, were designed to concentrate on procedural, not substantive questions.

Furthermore, HUD field program staff headed the monitoring teams. As the agency personnel responsible for overall performance, their incentives were to get programs running smoothly and in compliance with the regulations. Therefore, when HUD monitors encountered local problems, they usually tried to help communities meet the program requirements. Monitoring thus became less an exercise in measuring local performance than an opportunity to provide technical assistance.

Criticism of Local Performance

Because of the substantial discretion given to local governments in the program, the CDBG program attracted the attention of a broad range of researchers. The studies that resulted, from scholars, interest groups, and national associations concerned with housing and community development, almost universally condemned the program. Critics focused on two alleged shortcomings: first, that cities engaged in almost no real planning for the use of the money; and second, that CDBG funds were dispersed throughout communities, diminishing the program's opportunity to accomplish any real good, especially in easing the plight of the poor. Let us look at each of these points in more detail.

Absence of planning. In a study of six central cities from around the country, Victor Bach argued that cities had no coherent strategy for their CDBG funds. The program, instead, was little more than a collection of "piecemeal public works."[13] A coalition of public interest groups called local applications "municipal wish lists"[14] and Bernard J. Frieden and Marshall Kaplan condemned CDBGs as a "wasteful public works program with no evident purpose of its own."[15] Cities engaged in no real planning, the studies agreed, and as a result, the staff of the House Subcommittee on Housing and Community Development concluded after a survey of 138 communities, the local "plan" was little more than "a priced-out laundry list."[16]

Dispersion of funds. Many of the studies argued that, despite the act's injunction to give "maximum feasible priority" to the needs of the poor, local communities were in fact diverting funds away from the poor. One study by the National Association for the Advancement of Colored People (NAACP) found that a community had developed a marina.[17] In another study, the Southern Regional Council examined 26 cities in the South and alleged that one city spent $50,000 for a tennis complex in an affluent neighborhood while another city upgraded a stretch of road used by people going to a country club.[18]

The National Association of Housing and Redevelopment Officials (NAHRO) attempted to measure more systematically the
amount of money going to the poor. NAHRO surveyed the allocations made by 149 cities and broke the allocations down by the
median income of the census tract in which the projects were located. Their study reported that 51 percent of the funds in the first
year of the program went to low- and moderate-income tracts;* the
amount dropped to only 44 percent in the second year.[19] Taking
account of minor differences in methodology, the figures were generally consistent with similar studies done by the Southern California Association of Governments,[20] the National Urban League,[21]
the Brookings Institution,[22] and HUD.[23]

The result, according to one study, was a "scattergun" approach[24] with funds distributed throughout the city. According to
the National Urban League, "Expenditures under the Act have largely been diverted from the intended lower-income beneficiaries."[25]
One NAACP official concluded, "The poor in general have once
again become the victims of institutionalized discrimination."[26]

There are serious questions about how accurately some of
these studies characterized the program—questions even more important because the studies' criticisms of local performance forced
HUD away from its earlier permissive stance. Many of the studies
have three general problems.

First, they tend to concentrate only on the program's goal of
aiding the poor. As pointed out earlier, however, the CDBG program had multiple and sometimes conflicting goals (such as the goal
of aiding the poor vs. the goal of "spatial deconcentration" of the
poor). The program was not to be the successor to the War on
Poverty, yet in the absence of other antipoverty programs some interest groups chose to concentrate on this goal.

Second, the census tract method of analyzing the incidence of
benefits has a serious handicap: it assumes that the income level of
a census tract provides a good indicator of the benefits by income of
projects occurring within the tract. This assumption, however, is
questionable. Some projects in lower-income tracts may not benefit

---

*In this and similar studies, low-income tracts are defined as
tracts with a median family income of from 0 to 50 percent of the
median family income of the Standard Metropolitan Statistical Area
(SMSA) in which the city is located. Moderate-income tracts are
defined as tracts with median family income from 50 to 80 percent
of the SMSA median family income. Some alternative methods use
city median income instead of the SMSA amount.

lower-income residents, such as demolition and clearance of housing occupied by a poor family. Some projects in higher-income
census tracts may benefit a pocket of lower-income residents within
the tract, such as the rehabilitation of a block of badly deteriorated
homes. A project in a higher-income tract may also benefit lower-
income residents in a neighboring tract, such as the construction of
a new fire station to serve an adjoining poor neighborhood. Furthermore, citywide projects are characteristically excluded from this
method of analysis although some citywide projects directly benefit
the poor, such as improved health services. Other projects, such
as economic development, may in the long run bring new jobs to the
city and thus benefit the poor.

Narrative accounts of alleged discrimination against the poor—
the "horror stories" of marinas and tennis courts—are also suspect.
It is difficult to tell whether the circumstances they represent were
characteristic in the cities under study. The cities involved, furthermore, often defended their projects as a legitimate use of CDBG funds.
In the case of the tennis courts cited earlier, the city's government
angrily countered that the facilities were to be part of a comprehensive recreational complex to serve many poor black neighborhoods.
And, city officials reminded their critics, "Blacks play tennis,
too."[27]

The net effect of these methodologies was to underestimate
substantially the proportion of funds serving the lower-income residents and to focus debate on the program on only one goal, the goal
most easily quantified.

Unrealistic expectations. First Richard Nixon and then Gerald
Ford had argued that the "failures" of the earlier programs could be
remedied if only local communities had the funds relatively free from
federal controls. On signing the bill, Ford promised, "This new approach will put Federal funds to work on behalf of our cities and
towns far more effectively than before."[28] In the face of such rhetoric, the "failure" of the new program was hardly avoidable.

Many of the studies, furthermore, were prepared by organizations which significantly lost influence over urban policy as a result
of the decentralization strategy. Many were public interest groups
and national associations based in Washington and organized to lobby
there on behalf of their interests. Decentralization multiplied enor-
mously the number of decision-making points, making it that much
more difficult for the Washington-based lobbyists to influence policy.
Increased federal control of local governments was clearly in the
best interest of many of the monitoring groups.

All of this is not to say that the conclusions of these groups are
necessarily invalid. These studies, however, do not provide a clear
picture of how local governments performed.

The Formula Problem

The program included yet another source of controversy—this one between North and South—based in the original distribution formula. Beginning in fiscal year 1978, many older central cities would lose a substantial share of their grants. The 1974 legislation provided that those cities then receiving grants in excess of their formula entitlement would be "held harmless" against any decrease until fiscal year 1978. That is, cities would receive the higher amount of either their average categorical grant receipts or the formula entitlement. After the first three years of the program, all cities would be brought gradually to the formula amount.

For the older cities, declining cities, and cities that had been especially active in the previous categorical programs, the elimination of their "hold harmless" protection meant decreases, sometimes substantial, in their CDBG grants. For example, Rochester, New York, stood to lose 69.9 percent of its grant; Hartford, Connecticut, 68.8 percent, and Newark, New Jersey, 52.2 percent. The big losers tended to be concentrated in the Northeast and the Midwest. By contrast, some southern cities would receive huge windfalls. For example, Phoenix, Arizona, stood to gain a 726.7 percent increase; Dallas, Texas, 549.4 percent; and Fort Lauderdale, Florida, 436.4 percent. [29]

The formula question raised a difficult set of issues: directing financial support to the struggling northeastern and midwestern cities while maintaining support for the growing cities of the South which had legitimate development problems of their own. Congress's budget ceiling—too low to allow increases for everyone—further complicated the problem. [30]

Changes in the Program

The CDBG program as enacted contained a pair of problems: first, deciding the proper balance of authority between the federal and the local governments; and second, allocating the money fairly among the nation's cities. HUD attacked the authority problem through administrative action and Congress tackled the formula problem during the program's 1977 reauthorization.

Defining the federal role. During the Ford administration, HUD officials responded to the charges of local abuse by slowly but significantly increasing their control over local discretion. The Critical Issues Group issued Meeker Memos to provide more guidance to the field staff and to local communities on the review of applications, including "maximum feasible priority" and the eligibility of projects. HUD also issued a series of regulations in the Federal Register that, among other things, tightened the eligibility of proposed projects and established new procedures for filing applications and managing programs at the local level.

The flow of regulations seriously hurt the agency's early goal of reducing "red tape." Through July 1976, Meeker Memos totaled more than 100, and during the first 27 months of the program, HUD issued more than 200 pages of regulations in the Federal Register.*

A complete collection of CDBG program regulations, Meeker Memos, as well as the laws, executive orders and other requirements of the assurances filled eight two-inch think ring binders. HUD also began more extensive reviews of local applications, requiring communities to submit additional material to demonstrate that their proposed projects were eligible. The number of pages in local applications grew; cities spent more time preparing them and HUD spent more time reviewing them.[31]

The Carter administration came into office pledging even more stringent application reviews. HUD Secretary Patricia Roberts Harris promised to take "management steps to achieve the basic statutory objectives of our programs, especially those directed to the needs of low- and moderate-income people."[32] Assistant Secretary for Community Planning and Development Robert C. Embry, Jr. instructed HUD's field staff to subject local applications "to a thorough and meaningful review which goes beyond conformity with eligibility and technical requirements to consider the substance of what is proposed and how it serves statutory objectives."[33] HUD staff would examine each project, determine whether it met the act's goals and, if necessary, request further documentation from local communities to support the projects. The two officials made plain the agency's desire to strengthen its control over local performance. HUD sealed the break from its original goals by issuing in 1977 a booklet of "Consolidated Community Development Block Grant Regulations"—essentially a 150-page program handbook.

Changing the formula. Congressional debate on the formula issue in 1977 hinged on a war of computer printouts. Different partisans developed their own formulas, each accompanied by long lists of how much money each city would get under each alternative. Congress eventually adopted an approach developed by the Brookings Institution: a dual formula, with each city able to choose whichever formula gave them the larger grant. One formula was the original CDBG allocation strategy. The other included the age of housing

---

*This total includes both proposed and final regulations.

(50 percent), poverty (30 percent), and lag in population growth (20 percent). The first formula maintained the size of CDBG grants to the South, while the second formula assured the northeastern and midwestern cities that they would not lose money. The dual formula was not universally popular; some southern members of Congress argued that the new strategy simply maintained an unfair advantage that northeastern and midwestern cities had enjoyed since the beginning of the program. But Congress eventually approved the dual formula and insured that existing patterns of aid would not be upset.

UDAG. During the program's 1977 reauthorization, HUD fought successfully for a new adjunct to the CDBG program: Urban Development Action Grants (UDAGs). Congress agreed to provide $400 million for large projects in the most needy communities. The UDAGs would offer communities financial help for development opportunities that might arise. Furthermore, because the new program gave HUD discretion over which communities would receive the money, the UDAGs vested HUD with new authority to focus federal resources more precisely on federally determined projects.

ASSESSING LOCAL CAPACITY

The Problem of Performance

The changes in the program, especially HUD's increased supervision of local governments, serve only to reemphasize the problems discussed in Chapter 1. Wrapped up in the CDBG program are the issues of who—the cities or the federal government—should decide what needs are most important and which problems most deserve an infusion of federal aid. Also included are the questions of how the money should be administratively controlled: what forms of federal control there should be and what administrative capacity local governments possess.

Despite the changes in the program over its early years, it still maintained a large measure of discretion for local governments in how to spend the money. With the discretion came a large increase in administrative responsibility for executing the projects chosen. But the traditional criticisms of local governments remained, sometimes in the background, sometimes—as the result of some monitoring reports—across the front pages of newspapers.

Do cities have the capacity to plan and execute their projects effectively? Or, as the critics have argued, are cities so administratively weak and politically corrupt as to make effective project administration at the local level impossible?

In the coming chapters, we will examine two forms of local capacity. One is political capacity: the ability of local governments to respond to the needs of their citizens. The other is administrative capacity: the ability of local governments to execute the projects they have chosen. Our look at these two issues will help us to reach a judgment about how well the cities can respond to the challenge of the CDBG program.

Examining Performance

To examine the problem of local performance in the program, we will review the experiences of four Connecticut cities. The cities—Bridgeport, New Haven, New London, and Norwich—are few enough in number to allow for a careful, in-depth examination of their performances. The sample of cities is also matched to provide substantial variation on two variables likely to affect local performance—size and past experience with HUD's categorical programs—while controlling for potential confounding effects of other variables. Bridgeport and New Haven are relatively large cities compared with New London and Norwich. On the other hand, New Haven and New London were much more active in HUD's categorical programs than were Bridgeport and Norwich. (See Tables 2.2 and 2.3.)

TABLE 2.2

Sample of Cities

| | | Relative Experience | |
		High	Low
Relative Size	Large	New Haven	Bridgeport
	Small	New London	Norwich

We will probe the cities' performance during the first three years of the CDBG program, from August 1974 through August 1977. Conclusions are based predominantly on 65 interviews with officials most responsible for the program: the mayor or city manager in each city; local administrative officials who planned and administered

TABLE 2.3

Characteristics of the Cities

	Bridgeport	New Haven	New London	Norwich
Population (1970)	156,542	137,707	31,630	41,433
Median family income (1970)	$9,489	$9,031	$9,657	$9,768
Categorical Grant Program experience (fiscal year 1968-72) (amounts in millions of dollars)				
Urban renewal[a]	$6.7	$55.5	$24.7	$5.7
Model Cities	4.2	3.7	2.9	0
All other[b]	0.5	2.4	0.4	1.7
Total	$11.4	$61.6	$28.0	$7.4
CDBG entitlement (fiscal year 1975-77)[c] (amounts in millions of dollars)	$12.0	$54.0	$19.4	$4.4

[a]Including Neighborhood Development Program.

[b]Water and sewer facilities, open space, neighborhood facilities, rehabilitation loans, and public facilities loans.

[c]The fiscal years are federal fiscal years. Local fiscal years do not necessarily coincide. Furthermore, grants made by the federal government one fiscal year were generally counted by cities in their next fiscal year.

Source: U.S. Bureau of the Census, Census of Population and Housing, 1970; and U.S. Department of Housing and Urban Development files.

the projects; members of the city councils; members of citizen advisory bodies; and HUD officials at the area, regional, and central office levels.*

The study also draws on an examination of the written records: files maintained on each city by HUD; locally prepared documents submitted to HUD in compliance with program requirements; local files on the program; and local newspaper stories on the program.

In the next two chapters, we will study each city's experiences with the CDBG program. Each account will begin with a sketch of the city's development history and a survey of the forces that shaped its decisions on how to allocate the CDBG funds. Each account then will present two case studies of individual projects. These case studies have three features in common. First, each was a new project begun in the CDBG program. Second, the amount of money allocated to each project was a substantial share of the city's entitlement. Third, each case represented an attempt by the city to solve an important city problem.

There are important differences between the two cases for each city, however. Each city's first case is a "best case" in which the city was relatively successful in executing its plans. Each city's second case is a "worst case" in which the city experienced relatively serious execution problems. This "best case-worst case" approach (with "best" and "worst" defined solely in terms of a city's ability to fulfill its plans) has two advantages. First, the approach will allow us to examine the full range of the city's experiences rather than to concentrate on only its successes or its failures. Second, the approach will then allow us to examine what factors led to which outcomes and to explore the preconditions for success.

Chapters 5 and 6 will then explore in detail how the cities planned and executed their projects. In Chapter 7 we will reexamine what we have discovered and see what implications these discoveries might have for intergovernmental relations. But let us first move to the two cities with the greatest community development experience: New Haven and New London.

---

*The interviews consisted of open-ended questions directed at each official's area of involvement. Each interview lasted approximately one hour. All quotations not otherwise attributed come from these interviews.

NOTES

1. Housing and Community Development Act of 1974, 88 Stat. 633.

2. For a description of the events surrounding the passage of the bill, see the U.S. Advisory Commission on Intergovernmental Relations, Community Development: The Workings of a Federal-Local Block Grant (Washington, D.C.: March 1977), pp. 3-33.

3. Housing and Community Development Act of 1974, Sec. 105 (a).

4. Ibid., Sec. 105 (a) (8).

5. For a discussion of the goals of the act, see U.S. Congress, House, Committee on Banking, Finance and Urban Affairs, Community Development Grant Program, report by the staff of the Subcommittee on Housing and Community Development, Committee Print, 95th Cong., 1st sess., February 1977, pp. 3-16.

6. Memorandum to field staff, November 29, 1974.

7. Testimony of Floyd Hyde, former HUD Commissioner for Community Development, U.S. Congress, Senate, Committee on Banking, Housing and Urban Affairs, Community Development Block Grant Program, Hearings before the Committee on Banking, Housing and Urban Affairs, 94th Cong., 2d sess., 1976, p. 577.

8. See Robert L. Ginsberg, Mary K. Nenno, and Deena R. Sosson, NAHRO Community Development Monitoring Report: Year 1 Findings (Washington, D.C.: National Association of Housing and Redevelopment Officials, April 1976), p. 12; and testimony before the Senate Committee on Banking, Housing and Urban Affairs, Community Development Block Grant Program, especially by Richard Bach, p. 3; Peter Petkas, p. 27; and M. Howard Rienstra, pp. 35-36.

9. "Joint Explanatory Statement of the Committee of Conference," in U.S. Congress, House Committee on Banking and Currency, Compilation of the Housing and Community Development Act of 1974, Committee Print, 93rd Cong., 2d sess., October 1974, p. 303.

10. Testimony by Richard Bach before the Senate Committee on Banking, Housing and Urban Affairs, Community Development Block Grant Program, pp. 12-13.

11. Ginsberg et al., Community Development Monitoring Report, p. 12.

12. U.S. General Accounting Office, Meeting Application and Review Requirements for Block Grants under Title I of the Housing and Community Development Act of 1974 (June 23, 1976), pp. 10-11.

13. U.S. Congress, House, Committee on Banking, Finance and Urban Affairs, Housing and Community Development Act of 1977, hearings before the Subcommittee on Housing and Community

Development of the Committee on Banking, Housing and Currency, 95th Cong., 1st sess., 1977, p. 633.

14. Center for Community Change et al., "Community Development Block Grants," mimeographed (Washington, D.C.: 1976), p. 9.

15. Bernard J. Frieden and Marshall Kaplan, Community Development and the Model Cities Legacy (Cambridge, Mass.: Joint Center for Urban Studies of MIT and Harvard University, November 1976), p. 5.

16. Staff Report by the Subcommittee on Housing and Community Development, Community Development Block Grant Program, p. 32.

17. Frank DeStefano and Clay H. Wellborn, Aspects of Community Development Activities in Selected Localities (based upon information assembled by The Special Survey, Monitoring and Affirmative Action Project of the NAACP) (Washington, D.C.: The Library of Congress Congressional Research Service, June 28, 1976), pp. 4-5.

18. Raymond Brown with Ann Coil and Carol Rose, A Time for Accounting: The Housing and Community Development Act in the South (Atlanta: Southern Regional Council, March 1976), pp. 60-61.

19. Robert L. Ginsberg, "Second Year Community Development Block Grant Experience: A Summary of Findings of the NAHRO Community Development Monitoring Project (January 1977)," Journal of Housing 34 (February 1977): 81.

20. Southern California Association of Governments, SCAG Review of Second Year Housing and Community Development Title I Block Grant Applications (Los Angeles: Southern California Association of Governments, November 1976), p. 9.

21. National Urban League, "The New Housing Programs: Who Benefits?" mimeographed (New York: 1975), p. 15.

22. Sarah F. Liebschutz, "Community Development Block Grants: Who Benefits?" Paper prepared for delivery at the 1977 Annual Meeting of the American Political Science Association, Washington, D.C., September 1-4, 1977.

23. U.S. Department of Housing and Urban Development, Community Planning and Development, Office of Evaluation, Community Development Block Grant Program: Second Annual Report (Washington, D.C.: U.S. Government Printing Office, December 1976), pp. 24-25, 32-33.

24. Center for Community Change, "Community Development Block Grants," p. 9.

25. National Urban League, "The New Housing Programs," p. 1.

26. Letter from William R. Morris of the NAACP to Andrew Mott of the Center for Community Change, February 4, 1977, reprinted in House Committee on Banking, Finance and Urban Affairs, Housing and Community Development Act of 1977, p. 914.

27. Senate Committee on Banking, Housing and Urban Affairs, Community Development Block Grant Program, pp. 115–16.

28. U.S. Office of the Federal Register, Weekly Compilation of Presidential Documents 10 (Monday, August 26, 1974): 1060.

29. National Journal 9 (February 12, 1977): 242.

30. For a thorough discussion of the formula question, see Richard P. Nathan et al., Block Grants for Community Development (Washington, D.C.: U.S. Government Printing Office, January 1977), esp. pp. 75–240. See also a report by the U.S. General Accounting Office, Why the Formula for Allocating Community Development Block Grant Funds Should Be Improved (December 6, 1976).

31. See HUD, Second Annual Report, pp. 161–62.

32. Memorandum to CDBG recipients, April 15, 1977.

33. Memorandum to HUD field staff, April 1977.

3
NEW HAVEN AND NEW LONDON

NEW HAVEN

"Where Federal Dollars Pay Off"

In the mid-1950s, New Haven's Mayor Richard C. Lee seized the potential offered by HUD's categorical grant programs and began a determined effort to rebuild the city. As with many other New England cities, New Haven's financial and social base had slowly eroded as manufacturers moved to the South and many residents moved to the suburbs. But Lee became an aggressive grant seeker and won far more urban renewal funds per capita than any other mayor in the country.[1] He completely rebuilt the downtown area, replacing deteriorating houses and stores with a major shopping mall. He rehabilitated a quaint neighborhood full of distinguished but decaying brownstones and expanded the city's stock of public housing on sites scattered around the city. New Haven gained the reputation as the city "Where Federal Dollars Pay Off."[2]

Despite Lee's efforts, the city did not escape the turmoil that besieged the nation's major cities during the 1960s. The city had a riot in 1967 that did little physical damage but did shatter the city's confident self-image of a "model city." New Haven's antipoverty program, the model for the national War on Poverty, did not eliminate poverty and its Model Cities program left the model neighborhood, according to some critics, in worse shape than when the program began. The city looked to the new CDBG program as a new weapon to attack the city's difficulties.

Shortly after the passage of the program in 1974, Lee's successor, Bartholomew Guida, moved quickly to assert his control over the money. Within a month after the passage of the act, he established a six-member "Working Committee" of trusted advisors to supervise the program's planning and management. Guida pointedly excluded from the committee the heads of two city agencies—the City Plan Department and the Redevelopment Agency—which had become powerful under the categorical programs. To provide a citizen voice in the program, Guida also appointed representatives from many sectors of the community to a 17-member Citizen Participation, Advisory and Review Committee (CPAR). Guida instructed the citizens to review proposals for the $19.3 million in funds for the first year of the program and to make recommendations on how the money should be used.

CPAR held a long series of meetings through the fall and winter on the more than $40 million in requests for projects. But CPAR had no real staff, little substantive background in community development, and no objective criteria to guide it. In the end, the task of winnowing down the projects proved too big a job for the citizens' group.

LeRoy Jones, Guida's Development Administrator and a member of the Working Committee, did the job himself. He reviewed the proposed projects and after consulting with Guida assembled a draft application. Guida identified several projects for top priority: conversion of a downtown hotel into housing for the elderly (which we will explore in more detail in one of the case studies), a roof for a skating rink, and flood control for a neighborhood which had strongly supported him. Jones also reserved $2 million for public-service projects.

Jones faced his toughest decisions, however, on urban renewal projects. Redevelopment Agency officials for the first time faced competition from other city agencies for funds. Agency officials fought hard for the remaining funds and presented Jones with a long list of $150 million in incompleted projects. The agency stood no chance of getting even a significant portion of its requests but Jones did earmark most of the remaining first-year money for continuing the agency's acquisition, rehabilitation, and site improvement projects. Jones also decided to rely on the agency's staff to administer the 73 projects funded with first-year money.

The CPAR members received copies of Jones' proposal and Guida's thanks for their hard work but the material went to the Board of Aldermen—New Haven's city council—without any action by CPAR. The board itself held 13 hours of public hearings on the proposed application and heard hundreds of witnesses. Finally, the board decided to approve nearly all of the recommendations. But the aldermen also drew money from the application's contingency account to fund several public service projects whose supporters had been particularly vocal. (See Table 3.1 for a breakdown of the first-year application by function.)

TABLE 3.1

New Haven: Allocation of Money by Function
(in percentages)

Function	Year[a]			Total
	I (1975)	II (1976)	III (1977)	
Downtown renewal	7	0	0	2
Municipal services and equipment	0	0	0	0
Urban renewal	43	26	26	32
Housing rehabilitation	7	19	19	15
Neighborhood parks and facilities	4	3	4	4
Neighborhood public works	13	3	1	6
Social services	12	17	23	17
Planning and administration	12	17	24	17
Other	2	15[b]	3	7
Total	100	100	100	100
Amount (in millions of dollars)	$18.3	$18.7	$17.5	$54.5

[a] For local program year ending in calendar year shown.

[b] New Haven held a substantial reserve for economic development, particularly to assist a major local industry that needed to modernize its facilities.

Source: Derived from proposed activities in local applications.

Deliberations for the second-year application began only a few months later and provoked far more interest and conflict. Guida faced a Democratic primary election challenge from Alderman Frank Logue. Logue attacked Guida's CDBG plan, particularly the flood control project, as a failure to direct the money to the city's greatest needs.

Meanwhile, Guida faced a dispute within his administration over the proper use of CDBG funds. The city's neighborhood corporations—neighborhood-based antipoverty agencies—pressed for both new projects and for freedom from city hall control. Jones favored neither such a large role for public services nor the independence sought by the neighborhood corporations. Other members

of the mayor's staff, however, argued that the neighborhood corporations might prove valuable allies in the upcoming primary.
Guida agreed and a few weeks before the election distributed to
each neighborhood corporation a $28,000 grant from the first-year
contingency fund.

Logue defeated Guida in a close primary election and went on
to win the November general election. Upon taking office in January
1976 he immediately began work on the second-year application.
Logue abandoned CPAR and instead invited citizens to city hall to
discuss their needs and recommendations in a series of workshops.
More than 300 citizens attended the workshops, and from their
recommendations the Logue administration assembled its application.

Logue followed a dual strategy for the funds. First, he
pledged to renovate the neighborhoods instead of demolishing them.
He cut nearly in half the money the Redevelopment Agency had received the year before for its clear-and-redevelop approach. Instead, he argued for $3 million to save existing housing through
rehabilitation (another of the case studies). Second, he called for
a reorganization of CDBG public services. He contended that the
city should concentrate its money on two groups in the greatest
need—the young and the elderly—and said he would improve the
administration of the projects by coordinating them through a new
city agency, the Human Resources Administration.

The proposals drew large crowds at the aldermanic public
hearings. A Republican leader condemned Logue for eliminating
one of the redevelopment projects—Guida's flood control project—
and charged the change was a "political sanction" in retaliation for
the neighborhood's "failure to support him politically."[3] Logue's
public service proposals drew even larger crowds. Some groups
argued that different projects deserved funding. Others contended
that the amount budgeted for their projects should be increased or
at least maintained. The neighborhood corporations mounted particularly strong attacks and struggled to regain at least a measure
of the independence they had enjoyed under Guida.

The aldermen eventually approved most of Logue's proposals.
The Redevelopment Agency lost more than a third of its previous
year's budget as money for new rehabilitation projects tripled.
But the aldermen also took one-third of the contingency fund and
distributed it among several of the groups which had appeared
before them. Public service expenditures grew to $2.3 million, a
million-dollar increase from the first year. Even more dramati-
cally, the number of public service projects grew from 26 to 41.
Many of these projects did not fit Logue's priorities, but his key
projects nevertheless remained intact.

Logue used the citizen workshops again in the winter of 1977 as his staff began planning for the third year of the program. This year, however, the workshops drew few citizens, and city officials sometimes even sent student interns to represent the city. Citizens and city officials alike had realized that the important battle was before the aldermen.

Logue's proposals for the third year were little different than those of the previous year. He suggested another $2 million for the housing rehabilitation project and continued his attempts to impose a strategy on the public service projects. Again, however, the public service groups staged large demonstrations and forced the aldermen to reallocate the $17.5 million entitlement. The aldermen cut funds for several small hardware projects and added money to a wide range of public service projects, from the Concerned Citizens for the Deaf to the Puerto Rican Athletic Confederation. Public-service funds increased almost $1 million again, and the number of public service projects grew to 63. Even with the changes, though, the third-year application still showed the general shape of Logue's priorities.

Best Case: Neighborhood Preservation

One of the key planks of Logue's platform was the preservation and rehabilitation of existing housing. He based his position on philosophical conviction and financial necessity. First, federal financial support for the traditional, large-scale, concentrated public housing programs had disappeared. Second, there was little public support in New Haven for more of the public housing Lee had built. Finally, there was a growing public awareness of the integrity of the city's neighborhoods and an increasing willingness to try to save them.

Logue earmarked $3 million from the city's second-year entitlement to provide the "core element of a concentrated, comprehensive neighborhood preservation program aimed at upgrading the existing housing stock."[4] The project, he said, would include grants and low-interest loans "to make a dramatic and highly visible change in the physical condition of an area."[5]

In developing the project, Logue's planners faced three major strategic questions. First, should they focus the money on particular neighborhoods or should all areas of the city be eligible? Focusing would require a politically difficult decision to include some neighborhoods and exclude others. A citywide fund would avoid this problem but would also eliminate the neighborhood focus the mayor promised.

Second, if they chose the focused approach, should they concentrate the funds in the most seriously deteriorated neighborhoods or in the marginal, "grey" areas showing the first signs of deterioration? Some experts had argued that the grey-area strategy was both the most effective and most efficient course.[6] The individual properties generally were not so badly deteriorated that they required large expenditures for repair, so more properties could be renovated within a given project budget compared with a more seriously deteriorated neighborhood. The neighborhood as a whole, furthermore, was basically sound, so that fewer residences needed to be rehabilitated to "save" the neighborhood. On the other hand, the more seriously deteriorated neighborhoods were the areas of greatest need and the CDBG program was the only major source of funds for these needs.

Third, should the city use only its CDBG funds or should it attempt to increase the project budget by using CDBG money to attract private capital? With the involvement of the private sector would come the loss of some of the city's control over the program and an increase in administrative complexity. With a role for the private section would also come an increase in financial resources for the project.

A major tactical question also arose: which city agency should administer the project? The Redevelopment Agency had administered HUD's categorical rehabilitation programs* and had developed the staff and skills to do rehabilitation. But several members of Logue's staff questioned the commitment of Redevelopment Agency staff members to rehabilitation instead of traditional urban renewal. The alternative was to establish a new agency and hire a new staff to administer the project, but Logue was reluctant to tie up his pet project in the delays that would entail.

In the first months of the project, no one in city hall had clear responsibility for resolving the strategic questions. "It was a confused time," recalled John McGuerty, City Plan Director and Logue's Acting Development Administrator. "The delegation of responsibility was rather ludicrous." Gradually, Redevelopment Agency Executive Director William Donohue assumed leadership. Donohue had been working on a housing rehabilitation project since before Logue's election. Several city bankers had invited him to a meeting at which the bankers had discussed their common problems

---

*Under the provisions of HUD's Section 115 and Section 312 programs, New Haven rehabilitated 848 dwelling units in 393 structures, at a cost of $5.3 million (through May 1, 1976).

in some of the city's badly deteriorated neighborhoods, particularly the rising rate of default on mortgage loans. They suggested establishing a partnership between a consortium of banks and the city to rehabilitate some of the houses.

Donohue continued discussions with the bankers and by June they had developed a proposal for the Neighborhood Preservation project. The city would float a bond issue to provide $3 million in below-market-rate loans. CDBG funds would provide an additional $3 million pool for rehabilitation loans, security on the city's bonds, and acquisition and demolition of buildings unfit for rehabilitation. The banks would purchase the bonds to provide capital for the project and would supply staff experience.

Logue decided against the proposal. There was insufficient time, he said, to prepare a proper plan and to float the bonds. Some advisers also warned that the proposal entailed tricky legal and financial questions and argued that the city could not afford to jeopardize its AA bond rating on a project secured only by deteriorating housing stock.

McGuerty, Donohue, and their staffs went back to draw up a new proposal. The discussions this time included more city agencies—the Redevelopment Agency, the City Plan Department and its Economic Planning Unit, the Human Resources Administration, and the City Engineer's Office. The meetings, according to participants, were lengthy, and emotions ran high. Some individuals argued for what one staff member called a "dreamland program"; they saw Neighborhood Preservation as an opportunity to develop a major initiative for New Haven that integrated public services with a new approach to rehabilitation. Other individuals argued for a more conservative and practical approach to insure that the project would work.

Complicating the discussions were the private goals of some of the players. Housing in general and housing rehabilitation in particular were the specific responsibilities of no city official. The two key agencies both had other primary responsibilities rooted in their activities during the categorical grants: the Redevelopment Agency for land acquisition and disposition, the City Plan Department for comprehensive planning and esthetics. "Neighborhood Preservation," one staff member explained, "was really becoming a competitor for the programs the guys involved in the planning process were more interested in."

Logue finally insisted in September that his administrators produce a Neighborhood Preservation plan. The Redevelopment and City Plan staffs assembled a set of guidelines based on their previous meetings and finally, on September 30, 1976, Logue announced his Neighborhood Preservation project. He would establish

a new Office of Neighborhood Preservation within the Redevelopment
Agency, he said, to begin a concentrated rehabilitation project in
five "critical neighborhoods."* "We have opted to go where the
problems are; to seek the maximum effort in those areas," Logue
explained.[7] It was a "tough moral question," Logue recalled later:
putting the money into the more seriously deteriorated areas was
"riskier," but he found it "uncomfortable to say we have to write
off" some of the neighborhoods.

The new Office of Neighborhood Preservation would allocate
most of the money among the five neighborhoods by formula,†
reserving a small portion of the money for scattered rehabilitation
in other areas of the city. The office would also supervise the
establishment of Neighborhood Preservation Planning Teams in
each of the neighborhoods. Composed of local residents, the teams
would work with the office to decide which blocks would be eligible
for rehabilitation assistance. Logue's proposal concentrated money
on the rehabilitation of owner-occupied houses of from one to four
units, making grants of up to $5,000 available to homeowners who
met specified income limits.‡ The Office of Neighborhood Preservation could also make loans of $10,000 plus $5,000 for each unit up
to a total of four; the loans would be made at an interest rate of
3 percent with up to 20 years to repay.** Logue explained:

> The intent of this program is to launch an emphatic,
> fast-moving, concentrated, comprehensive attack
> on the blighting and deteriorated conditions encroach-
> ing on the city landscape and threatening the strength
> and stability of our neighborhoods.[8]

Logue's announcement received a mixed reaction. The New
Haven Register doubted whether the project would work. "Unless

---

*The neighborhoods were: Hill, Fair Haven, Newhallville,
Dwight, and Dixwell. Each of the neighborhoods had previously
been the target of urban renewal projects, and the Hill neighborhood
was the target neighborhood for the Model Cities program.

†The formula took account of the total number of dwelling units
in the neighborhood, the number of one- to four-unit structures, and
the condition of the neighborhood's housing stock.

‡For example, a family of four needed an income of less than
$12,850 to be eligible.

**Absentee owners were also eligible for the project, but
they were not eligible for grants and the interest rate on the loans
was 6 percent.

financial and human resources are adequately marshaled," the
paper said, "the outcome could amount to nothing more than
tokenism."[9] The bankers were surprised that Logue's project did
not include them and wondered whether the city would "be spread-
ing the money too thin to make much impact." A bank president
concluded, "they are just going to throw good money after bad."[10]

The new Office of Neighborhood Preservation worked hard to
get the project moving swiftly. The office's staff held a long series
of meetings with residents of the neighborhoods to explain the
project and to assist the Preservation Teams in choosing the blocks
that would receive aid. By the end of January, 150 city residents
had joined the teams and had selected their targets.

Not surprisingly, the selection proceeded neither smoothly
nor unanimously. There were strong and sometimes heated arguments within the teams, and on occasion the office suggested
changes in the teams' priorities. Furthermore, the office's
director explained, when the teams "selected one street and didn't
select another street, they offended people." It was hard, one
office staff member explained, to tell an interested resident that
even though he met the project's income guidelines and his neighbor
around the corner was participating, he could not be given a grant
or a loan because he was not living on a priority street.

Nevertheless, Logue was pleased with the project. In
February 1977, he asked the Board of Aldermen to allocate an
additional $2 million for the project from third-year CDBG funds:

> Our Office of Neighborhood Preservation has to date
> been an unqualified success. We have begun the pro-
> cess of building up, rather than tearing down, our
> neighborhoods, and we are now beginning to see the
> improvements in homes made possible by the Neigh-
> borhood Preservation program.[11]

By the end of June, the office had committed $1.5 million of the $3
million total to 316 dwelling units in 187 different structures, an
average of $8,000 for each structure.[12] But in addition to the
rehabilitation, the project also had an important political effect.
One office member explained that the project had established a new
channel of communications between the city and the neighborhoods:

> There's nobody at war with us at this time. That's
> the key. The neighborhood committees are strong
> and they're not afraid to push us. They're not afraid
> to ask questions. That's the real strength of this
> program.

Worst Case: Hotel Taft Rehabilitation Project

Once the proud centerpiece of New Haven's downtown, the Hotel Taft closed its doors in October 1973 after years of declining patronage. Named after the head of a local private school (the brother of the President of the United States), for 61 years the Taft had hosted the greats of the theater world who came to New Haven for pre-Broadway tryouts at the Shubert Theatre next door. With the decline of New Haven's downtown and the growth of newer suburban motor inns, however, the ornate marble and brick hotel drew fewer and fewer customers until its owners eventually shut it down.

As New Haven began planning the use of its CDBG funds in 1974, Jay Vlock, the president of a center-city housing development for the elderly, suggested to Mayor Bart Guida that the city use the money to convert the old Taft into housing for the elderly. The idea intrigued Guida and he asked several city agencies to draw up plans.

In early January 1975, the Redevelopment Agency presented him with a plan. The Redevelopment Agency would acquire the property and, with the City Plan Commission, work out the architectural and legal questions. Then the New Haven Development Corporation, a nonprofit organization of city businesspeople, would buy the old hotel, renovate it, and operate it as a tax-paying, nonprofit enterprise. The new Taft would provide 300 units of housing, a senior citizens center, and 14,000 square feet of stores on the bottom floors. City officials also hoped to make improvements to the Shubert Theatre and to tie the complex together with a network of elevated walkways. The Redevelopment Agency's plan concluded:

> With New Haven's shortage of vacant land, it is essen-
> tial to upgrade existing uses where possible. The Hotel
> Taft-Adams complex contains not only structurally
> sound buildings that are feasible to rehabilitate, but
> buildings that are an important part of our City's
> background. [13]

Financing for the $7.3 million plan would come through a complex arrangement among the city, the State of Connecticut, and HUD. First, the State's Housing Site Development Program would pay two-thirds of the cost of site acquisition, estimated by the Redevelopment Agency at $1.75 million. Second, the city would supply its one-third share of site acquisition costs—about $583,000—from its first-year CDBG entitlement. Finally, Vlock reported that

HUD's new Section 8 rent subsidy program would provide assistance to the elderly residents and therefore insure the profitability of the completed project. The New Haven Chamber of Commerce announced its "wholehearted" support for the project and Vlock added:

> This project started as an idea. But it is now moving toward reality through the enthusiasm of the city, the Redevelopment Agency, the state, the architects and the New Haven Development Corporation. . . .
>   What we want is for this project to provide a central meeting place for the elderly of the greater New Haven area where they can be housed, helped, entertained, loved, and cared for. After all, it's only fitting that this generation of elderly should provide the humane rebirth of this historic and most central part of the city.[14]

HUD approved the city's application for CDBG funds, including its local share for acquisition and site development. When the agency announced its allocation for Section 8 subsidies, however, New Haven received funds to subsidize the rental payments on only 234 units. Not only was the amount less than the 300 needed for the Taft project, but even if the city had received another 66 units, it would have been politically difficult to concentrate its entire allocation on a single project. Furthermore, although the legislative authority remained, the state had made no financial commitments to the Housing Site Development Program since the early 1970s. New Haven's application proved no exception. The financial plans for the project disintegrated.

In addition, some members of the city administration increasingly doubted that the Taft would serve the elderly well. Some staff members argued that the project would lend little vitality to the neighborhood after dark; the elderly would be fearful to venture out and would become "virtual prisoners," one staff member feared. Furthermore, without the Section 8 subsidies, the apartments would prove too expensive for the lower-income elderly for whom they were intended. City Plan Director John McGuerty concluded that the planned conversion would be "abysmal."

Guida and his advisers decided to go ahead with the plans to convert the Taft into apartments, but they realized that they would have to make three major changes in their plans. First, without sufficient Section 8 subsidies and with the concerns of the planners for the viability of housing for the elderly on the site, the project would have to accommodate a different tenant mix. Second, without the subsidies and without financial help from the state, the city would have to finance the entire project itself. The only source of "local" funds was the CDBG program. Finally, even though New Haven received an $18 million entitlement from HUD for the first year, there were many other competing demands for the funds.

Guida therefore decided to reduce the scale of the project. Instead of attempting a comprehensive transformation of the entire neighborhood, the city would instead concentrate only on rehabilitating the Taft. Guida also decided to fund the city's costs entirely from the CDBG program. He amended the first-year application and increased the amount budgeted for acquisition from $580,000 to slightly more than $1 million. A few months later, the Redevelopment Agency was ready to make an offer to purchase the Taft from its owners. But the $1 million the city could offer was far less than the $2,5 million price the owners had advertised. The deal fell apart.

As Guida left office, six months after the end of the first CDBG program year, the money lay virtually unspent.* Frank Logue on taking office told Redevelopment Agency Executive Director Donohue that he favored the conversion project. But he made plain that he wanted a carefully developed plan that would minimize the city's risks.

Donohue conferred with several interested firms and met finally with officials of the Starrett Housing Corporation. The Starrett officials had come to New Haven to discuss the possible acquisition of another property, but Donohue pointed to the Taft and its key location near the city's historic green. Starrett had been working on other hotel conversion projects, and Donohue convinced the company's analysts that they could turn the Taft into a profitable apartment complex.

On April 7, 1977, Logue announced Starrett's plans for a $6.3 million conversion of the Taft into 208 apartments. The units, he said, would be spacious and would represent some of the finest housing in the Northeast. The apartments would range in size from studios to two bedrooms while commercial and restaurant facilities would occupy the ground floor. Starrett, Logue explained, would apply to the Federal Housing Administration (FHA) for mortgage insurance. After the firm secured FHA approval, the Redevelopment Agency would acquire the property and sell it to Starrett. The

---

*The city had spent about $10,000 for engineering studies and drawings. In addition to the $1 million for acquisition, the city had also budgeted $300,000 for improvements to the neighborhood that likewise remained unspent.

corporation would then fund the renovation with the assistance of the State of Connecticut Housing and Finance Authority.

The plan attracted substantial local support. "We feel the Taft proposal is very exciting," Logue said[15] and the New Haven Register editorially agreed: "The city's version of a rehabilitated Taft would be a fine asset to the city—perhaps as much of a credit as the hotel was in its heyday."[16] Another local newspaper applauded the project, calling it "a move as much symbolic as substantive."[17]

Starrett promptly filed application for mortgage insurance with the FHA. The FHA, however, replied with a series of questions about the project's costs, centering particularly on the cost for each apartment and the Taft's eventual marketability. Starrett prepared responses to the FHA's questions and conducted additional marketing studies, but at the conclusion of the second year of New Haven's CDBG program the Taft was still vacant and the start of construction was nowhere in sight. "A vacant building is the worst thing to have," Donohue concluded. "It's a symbol of futility, of a sick situation."

NEW LONDON

The Whaling Port

By the middle of the nineteenth century, New London was the third largest whaling port in the country and had also developed a sizable shipbuilding industry. As sailing disappeared from New England commerce at the end of the century, New London replaced it with shops and offices that soon made the city the leading commercial center of southeastern Connecticut. After World War II, however, businesses gradually left the downtown area for the newly developing suburbs, and the quality of the city's housing deteriorated.

New London's officials aggressively sought funds to eliminate the growing slums to the north and south of the central business district. The city cleared large tracts of land and built new developments of public housing. In an effort to improve the city's commercial life, local officials attempted to improve road access to the downtown area and extended the boundaries of one of the projects to include part of the city's major shopping area. They used federal funds to transform several blocks of city streets into a pedestrian shopping mall. Meanwhile, city officials launched a Model Cities program to serve a growing low- and moderate-income population.

Despite the city's efforts, however, the central business district showed no signs of stabilizing. Large parts of the urban renewal projects remained empty tracts of land. Many local residents and merchants viewed the pedestrian mall as a failure, and few new stores showed interest in locating downtown. The city's political leaders looked to the CDBG program as a source of money to try new solutions.

Late in 1974, New London's city manager created a small Office of Community Development, staffed by two planners, to prepare the city's application and oversee the implementation of CDBG projects. The city council also appointed a nine-member Citizens Advisory Council (CAC), composed of one member from each of the city's seven voting districts and two at large, to review the requests for CDBG funds and to make recommendations.

City agencies proposed an enormous number of projects, ranging from a new fire station to a $9 million system of improvements to the city's water system. New London officials also held a series of six well-attended neighborhood meetings that produced still more suggestions. The Office of Community Development in all collected more than $50 million in proposals for the city's $6.1 million entitlement.

The CAC was at first overwhelmed. Not only was there an enormous number of projects, but the CAC had only six weeks to make its recommendations. After a long series of meetings, however, the CAC produced a set of recommendations focused on public works, neighborhood improvements, and public services. At first they considered excluding the Redevelopment Agency from CDBG funds because of widespread dissatisfaction over the agency's past performance. The CAC finally recommended a small budget for redevelopment, much smaller than the agency had requested.

The Office of Community Development prepared its own list of recommendations. Their version concurred with many of the choices made by the CAC but set a larger allocation for the Redevelopment Agency. The city council then held its own series of hearings to gather public opinion on the two sets of recommendations. The council finally agreed with most of the office's recommendations. The councilors allocated one-third of the money for continuation of several urban renewal projects by the Redevelopment Agency and set aside $660,000 for a housing rehabilitation project. The council members also earmarked $170,000 for a new fire station (one of the case studies we will explore shortly) and nearly $1.4 million for public service projects (see Table 3.2).

When the office collected new suggestions a few months later for second-year projects, the requests totaled $18 million, substantially less than the first year but still three times more than the city's entitlement. The Redevelopment Agency this year proposed a major renewal project for Bank Street, a declining downtown commercial area (and another of the cases we will examine). Again the CAC held a long series of hearings and again the CAC opposed the Redevelopment Agency. New London should allocate its money to improving its deteriorating housing, they said, instead of the Redevelopment Agency projects. But again the Office of Community Development sided with the Redevelopment Agency.

TABLE 3.2

New London: Allocation of Money by Function
(in percentages)

	Year[a]			
	I (1975)	II (1976)	III (1977)	Total
Downtown renewal	7	29	36	24
Municipal services and equipment	17	13	7	12
Urban renewal	25	6	0	10
Housing rehabilitation	11	11	19	14
Neighborhood parks and facilities	9	4	6	6
Neighborhood public works	4	6	1	3
Social services	21	18	21	20
Planning and administration	5	12	9	9
Other	1	1	1	1
Total	100	100	100	99[b]
Amount (in millions of dollars)	$6.1	$6.9	$6.4	$19.4

[a] For local program year ending in calendar year shown.
[b] Total does not add due to rounding.
Source: Derived from proposed activities in local applications.

This year, however, public service agencies dominated the city council's hearings. The CAC, citing the projected decrease in New London's entitlement to zero by 1981, had recommended cuts in the budgets for the public service projects.* One council member, Richard Uguccioni, agreed and warned that the city could not continue to fund these projects indefinitely from the CDBG program and would not use local tax revenue to sustain them. "The ones that don't stand on their own two feet and show some professionalism," Uguccioni said, "are going to be out in the cold as far as I'm concerned."[18]

As the council prepared to decide, 70 persons crowded into the small council chambers to make last minute appeals for funds. The council responded by splitting an additional $44,000 among five public service projects. The council also decided to side with the Office of Community Development against the CAC and approved the Bank Street proposal. They completed the application by continuing most of the projects from the previous year.

The council's actions left CAC members angry. One member complained, "We spent two and a half weeks of intensive study only to find a major portion of our recommendations ignored by the council." Another member said, "I think the council has been unresponsive to the community in subjecting itself to political pressure in making decisions."[19]

The conflicts intensified in the third-year allocation process. The CAC again argued for substantial cuts in many public service projects, less money for Bank Street, and more money for rehabilitation. The Office of Community Development saw the Bank Street project as the key to the city's renewal and again opposed the CAC. But once again, it was the public services budget that attracted the most attention. A spokesman for the Spanish-American Cultural Organization (SACO) demanded that the city council restore cuts made from his $55,000 request:

> We don't deal with buildings. We are not redeveloping facades. We are not working with veneer. We are dealing with people.
>
> There are $6 million in Community Development funds. SACO wants $20,000 [more]. There are 4,000 Hispanic people in the city of New London. That is 12 percent of the population. Proportionally, it is our right to receive not $40,000 but $720,000.[20]

---

*After Congress amended the CDBG formula in 1977, however, New London's entitlement declined to $1.2 million.

To satisfy SACO and other public service agencies that had packed the council galleries with their supporters, the council cut $80,000 from the Bank Street allocation and redistributed the money to six public service projects—including SACO. But council member George G. Spreace warned the agencies, "It is fortunate that we are able to accommodate you to this extent. But I caution you that there will be considerably less money in the next several years."[21] In the third year of the CDBG program, however, Bank Street and the public service projects dominated the local agenda.

Best Case: Bank Street Revitalization Project

Until the mid-1950s, a broad collection of restaurants, stores, banks, doctors, and dentists made downtown New London a bustling center of prosperity. But with the last years of the 1950s, the development of new shopping centers in the suburban towns drew shoppers away from the downtown area. Meanwhile, the problems of crime, deteriorating housing, and the attractiveness of the new stores in the shopping centers led the downtown department stores, one by one, to close and relocate.

The decline of the downtown area as a shopping district created tax problems for New London and left rows of empty buildings. Real estate assessments along State Street, the principal shopping avenue, dropped by more than $500,000 from the mid-1950s to the mid-1970s.[22] Bank Street— once the center of New London's whaling industry and later part of its central shopping district—became occupied with pornographic book stores, bars, and prostitutes. A once-proud Bank Street theater, formerly the home of vaudevill and silent movies, showed X-rated movies in the early 1970s until it eventually closed.

Earlier efforts to reverse the trend had produced only limited success. City officials had extended the boundaries of one urban renewal project to include the center of the shopping district and had transformed the street into Captain's Walk, a pedestrian shopper's mall with a cobblestone walkway and colorful kiosks. The city had also attempted to improve the traffic flow through the narrow, tangled streets that dated from the city's whaling days and had built a new parking garage. The projects produced no quick improvements, and while merchants debated the effects of the project on their businesses, public confidence in downtown New London continued to decline.

In December 1975, planning consultants to the New London Redevelopment Agency proposed a three-part plan to revitalize the Bank Street area. The consultants suggested:

■ acquisition and demolition of deteriorated buildings along Bank Street;

    ■ expansion of downtown parking by developing new lots; and,

    ■ extension of another street to improve the traffic flow through the downtown area.

These three elements, the consultants argued, would solve traffic problems, increase parking, eliminate blighted buildings, improve access to the waterfront behind Bank Street, and, they hoped, attract shoppers back downtown.

The Redevelopment Agency requested $2.88 million in second-year CDBG funds for the Bank Street project. The Citizens Advisory Committee recommended that the project receive only $1.5 million and argued that the city should use the difference to expand the city's housing rehabilitation project. The city council eventually compromised on an allocation of $1.9 million.

In February 1976, the city council approved detailed plans for the Bank Street Project. The council's plans, however, contained two elements that enraged the area's merchants. First, to improve traffic flow, the council proposed making Bank Street one-way. Second, instead of demolishing deteriorating buildings, the council established a $750,000 fund for the subsidy of interest rates on rehabilitation loans for the buildings.

Sixteen of the merchants signed a petition protesting the plan to make the street one-way, fearing that one-way traffic would make it too easy to drive through the area without stopping to shop. One merchant explained, "You need revitalization bringing back life. But bringing back life to downtown does not have as its main thrust building by-pass arteries around the downtown area."[23] Instead the merchants called on the council to demolish the worst of the buildings in the area and to "zone out the sleazy bars, the peddlers of pornography and the massage parlors."[24] One city council member suggested a more drastic solution: have the Redevelopment Agency buy the buildings and "bomb them out."[25]

The merchants' opposition forced the council back from the one-way street plan. But as the merchants built support for the demolition of some Bank Street properties, groups interested in the preservation of the buildings organized. They told the council that demolition would destroy important relics of the city's whaling past. The head of one group, New London Landmarks, explained:

This is a real nineteenth-century seaport street. It's the only street in the city that authentically illustrates the city's whaling and maritime past. . . .

> The street has to be treated as a whole. You
> can't say you are going to save some buildings and
> not save others and still retain the personality and
> history of the street. [26]

Instead, he suggested that New London follow the example of New-
port and Providence, Rhode Island, which had restored their
historic buildings to build a tourist industry.

In May, the city's planning board approved revised Bank
Street plans, proposed by the Redevelopment Agency, that sided
with the merchants. Board member Charles Curtin cast the lone
dissenting vote, saying:

> I'll lever support a plan calling for buildings to be
> torn down until someone proves to me that there are
> structural problems with them. Good, bad, or in-
> different, there's plenty of activity on Bank Street,
> but there won't be any if those buildings are torn
> down. [27]

But board member Raymond Moreau sharply disagreed:

> We don't need any more tax-free historic buildings in
> this city—we can't afford any more. The people who
> are arguing to preserve the buildings for their historic
> value are free-loaders and they can go to hell as far
> as I'm concerned. [28]

Meanwhile, the staff of the Redevelopment Agency met with
30 merchants from Bank Street. Agency planners explained that
the historic preservation forces could stall the project for perhaps
two years if they decided to take legal action against the demolition
plans. Although most merchants expressed hope that the buildings
would eventually be torn down, they agreed informally to proceed
with the other parts of the plan and to give the demolition plans
further study. The Redevelopment Agency then developed a modi-
fied plan that would create a program of loan subsidies to encourage private rehabilitation of Bank Street buildings. The agency
also agreed to conduct further architectural studies of nine Bank
Street buildings previously scheduled for demolition to determine
their feasibility for rehabilitation.

Two months later, New London contracted with Halcyon
Limited, a Hartford-based consulting firm, to devise a new and

imaginative strategy for New London's downtown area.* Halcyon returned with an elaborate strategy designed to use New London's "unique historical character . . . to flavor the image of the City which will be developed in the rejuvenation process."[29]

The basic theme for New London's rejuvenation, Halcyon said, should be "turning the City back towards its major natural amenity": the waterfront.[30] Halcyon proposed:

- development of City Pier at the foot of Captain's Walk;
- construction of a promenade for strolling and sitting along the waterfront;
- erection of a raised boardwalk behind Bank Street for shops, cafes, and bistros; and,
- rehabilitation of the storefronts along Bank Street to reflect the city's whaling heritage.

The new ideas, Theodore Amenta of Halcyon explained, are "flamboyant, aesthetic improvements designed to make the area more attractive for [private] investment."[31]

The Redevelopment Agency revised its Bank Street plans to match Halcyon's recommendations, earmarking $2.1 million in second-year CDBG funds and $3.2 million from the third year. The city council, however, opposed the boardwalk and said the ideas involved too much money to proceed without extensive public input. The Redevelopment Agency reluctantly concurred and eliminated the boardwalk from its plans.

Halcyon's Amenta countered with a public campaign for the boardwalk. "Pivotal to the whole plan is the boardwalk," he said. "This is the life-giving thing."[32] At a well-attended public hearing in late October, the downtown merchants agreed that the boardwalk would help to draw people back downtown again. "The boardwalk has definite possibilities," one council member concluded after the meeting. Another concurred: "Something has to be done to show confidence in the city."[33] As a result of Amenta's efforts and public support for the boardwalk, the city council voted the boardwalk back into the project.

---

*Halcyon had developed a national reputation for powerful concepts and quick results. In Hartford, a year of conventional marketing efforts had produced only one tenant for Aetna Life and Casualty's Civic Center Shops, a 220,000-square-foot downtown shopping plaza. Aetna hired Halcyon and within ten months the firm had leased the entire property through a combination of public image building and aggressive marketing. In New York, Citibank hired Halcyon to lease a three-story shopping mall within the bank's new 50-story headquarters.

The staff of the Redevelopment Agency attempted to begin work on the project. The lack of commitment by their oversight board, the Redevelopment Commission, however, combined with the board's overzealous supervision of the details of the project to delay the staff members' work. Long used to dealing with the acquisition and demolition of substandard properties, some members of the commission were "not totally committed to the project," according to one city official. The commission also insisted on approving the minutiae of project plans, resulting in "too much interference in the administration of the agency." "No discretion seems to be left to the administrators to get the job done," a city official concluded.

Nevertheless, the Redevelopment Agency staff got the project moving. By the end of July 1977, rehabilitation work on two Bank Street structures had been completed and another half-dozen jobs were out to bid. With support from project loans, a new restaurant opened nearby in the city's renovated railroad station. New London rebuilt its city pier as part of the project and then attracted a major festival of sailing ships to the pier.* First the festival and later a dance for teenagers drew thousands of people back downtown. Merchants found "a noticeable increase in business," one city official said, and "there is a complete change in attitude." As one local newspaper columnist noted happily after the festival,

> Captain's Walk, the area around the Soldiers and
> Sailors Monument and the City Pier looked like some-
> thing out of the halcyon days of the New London
> whaling era—or the way we hoped it might have
> looked. [34]

Worst Case: South End Fire Station

Since the early 1970s, New London had been reorganizing its system of fire protection. The city had built a new fire station in the North End and planned another new station in the South End to consolidate two older fire companies. One station, the Pequot Engine Company, was an old and deteriorating structure owned by the company's volunteer firemen and leased to the city. The building was too small for modern fire equipment—the fire department removed the flashing light from one truck to squeeze it in and a new

---

*The Sail Festival was largely the work of the city's maritime consultant, hired with money from the city's second-year entitlement.

truck on order would not fit inside. Laborers from the Works
Project Administration had built the other station, the Ockford
Hose Company, in 1933. The station was still in adequate condition, but its location at the bottom of a steep hill hindered the
prompt dispatch of fire equipment.

New London's city officials saw the CDBG program as a way
to construct the needed new South End Fire Station without raising
taxes or increasing the city's bonding.* The Citizens Advisory
Council recommended an expenditure of $450,000 from first-year
CDBG funds for the station, but the administration recommended
that the funding be spread over the first and second years of the
program. The city council approved $170,000 from first-year
funds for design work and planned to allocate the money needed for
construction from second-year funds.

The preliminary design work proceeded without the selection
of a site. In requesting $305,000, in second-year CDBG funds,
City Manager C. Francis Driscoll recommended a site adjacent to
a dairy. The City Council's Public Safety Committee, however,
favored Toby May Field, a municipal park a short distance from
Long Island Sound Beaches. Because the city already owned the
property, the council members argued, building the fire station in
the park would save the city the cost, estimated at $100,000, of
acquiring the dairy site or other private property.

Members of Congregation Beth El synagogue, located next to
the park, objected to the council's plan. The city had bought the
land from the synagogue in 1953, and the synagogue claimed an
unwritten agreement with the city in transferring the property: the
land would only be used for a school or for recreational facilities.
The president of the congregation told the council that "we decided
to sell [the property] without the deed restrictions and rely on the
good faith of the city."35 He called on the city to honor its commitment. Residents of the neighborhood—mostly middle- and
high-income persons with single-family houses—also objected to
construction of the fire station. They argued that the street was

---

*The city's police station was also badly deteriorated, and
local officials searched for funding to construct a new building.
Due to the peculiarities in the CDBG regulations, however, the
construction of fire facilities was an eligible expenditure while
building a police station was not. HUD looked on fire stations as
neighborhood improvements, while the agency saw police stations
as benefiting a broader constituency.

too congested already and that taking a corner of the park would
seriously damage the recreational facilities.

Two officers of the city's professional firefighters union
appeared before the council to argue for the site. Toby May Field,
they said, was the most centrally located property for the new fire
station and it was on a major thoroughfare. Furthermore, they
pointed to two recent studies of New London's fire protection system that recommended the consolidation of the city's South End fire
equipment at the Toby May Field stie, one by the International Fire
Chiefs Association and the other by the Insurance Services Office,
a risk-rating agency for the insurance industry.

Members of the New London Taxpayers Association joined
the firefighters in support for the site. Using the city-owned
property would save the city site acquisition costs and would improve the city's fire protection, they told the council. "It would be
politically sound" to put the fire station elsewhere, one member of
the association contended, "but what is politically good is not necessarily in the best interest of the city."[36]

Even though the city had not yet selected a site, the Citizens
Advisory Council now faced a decision on allocating money for construction from the second-year entitlement. In the face of overwhelming citizen opposition, they recommended no money. But despite the citizen council's recommendation and threats from citizens
of a referendum on the fire station question, the city council voted
4-2 in favor of the Toby May Field site and earmarked $305,000 in
second-year funds. One council member defended the council's
action, saying, "Regardless of where we put the firehouse, the
neighbors won't like it."[37]

The city's newspaper, however, editorially called the decision a "foolish error" and asked:

> Why is the New London City Council so intent upon
> building the South End firehouse on part of Toby
> May Field? Despite obvious and widespread public
> opinion to the contrary and plenty of solid logic argu-
> ing against the plan, the Council seems bent on
> destroying one of the city's few remaining recrea-
> tional areas.[38]

And a letter to the newspaper's editor said, "In my opinion, it is a
crime against the present and future residents of New London to
permit the votes of four city councilors to stand against the out-
spoken sentiments of the people."[39]

Meanwhile, the city hired a consulting firm to prepare the required environmental impact statement for the project.* In March, the firm reported that the fire station would not have an adverse impact on the environment. The report angered opponents of the project and triggered a barrage of complaints to the city council and to HUD.† The complaints forced the council in May to order further studies of potential noise and traffic problems. But the council, hoping that the limited study would satisfy the critics, resisted pressure for a more extensive six-month survey. Even the limited study, city officials felt, was "investigative overkill."

The studies did not pacify the residents. They began collecting signatures in June to force a referendum on the fire station question and within two weeks had obtained 1,200 names on their petitions. But the city council used a parliamentary maneuver to render the referendum moot, replacing the original fire station budget (against which the citizens directed their petition campaign) with a new, slightly smaller budget.

The new environmental studies ordered by the city council reported that the Toby May Field site would pose no environmental problems. The consultant who had prepared the city's earlier report said that the fire equipment would have no trouble threading through the streets in the neighborhood, even during the busy beach season. An acoustics engineer loaned to the city from the U.S. Navy's Naval Underwater Systems Center in New London reported that the fire station would create no significant noise problems. In fact, he said, a fire engine leaving the station without its siren on would be indistinguishable from background noise. Although citizen groups still complained and threatened injunctions against construction, the reports effectively ended debate on the environmental effects of the fire station on Toby May Field.

The plans then went to the city's Board of Finance which, by the city's charter, had to approve all expenditures. But in September the board stymied the council by voting against the fire station appropriation 0-3-1. As one member explained, "I want a firehouse. But

---

*Local governments performed the environmental reviews required by the National Environmental Policy Act of 1969 of all projects involving federal funds.

†HUD's response to citizen complaints in the CDBG program was to explain to the citizen that it is the responsibility of the local government to deal with substantive questions about the local program. The agency then has sent a copy of the complaint to the city and has requested that the city respond promptly to it.

I think there should be a referendum. The people should have the opportunity to vote for it. I don't like all that playing around by the City Council."[40]

The board's action stopped plans for the Toby May Field site and in late September the city council began searching for an alternative site. The council voted to have a property nearby the park appraised but neighbors of that property immediately began a petition drive against the new site. One resident explained, "A firehouse doesn't belong in a highly residential area. I realize that the street might be a convenient one for a firehouse, but they just shouldn't put one here."[41] Faced with such strong opposition from his neighbors, the owner withdrew the property from consideration even though the city had already spent the money to have it appraised.

Faced with another dead end, the council reexamined an earlier proposal to purchase the Pequot Hose Company property and consolidate the city's South End fire services there, but members of the rival Ockford Hose Company began circulating a petition against that proposal. With no other alternatives viable, the council returned in January 1977 to consideration of the Toby May Field site. One week later, however, the Board of Finance again rejected an appropriation for the site.

By the end of the second year of New London's CDBG program in June 1977, the city was no closer to the construction of the South End Fire Station than it was when the CDBG program began. In October, the city council decided to reallocate the fire station funds—except for a $5,000 planning reserve—into the city's parks rehabilitation program.

CONCLUSION

Only a handful of U.S. cities had been more active for their size in HUD's categorical programs than New Haven and New London. Because of the CDBG program's hold harmless provision, this left the two cities with an extraordinarily large CDBG entitlement. The categorical programs, however, left a larger legacy. The cities had a long agenda of uncompleted renewal projects and had politically powerful redevelopment agencies who meant to finish them. The cities also had vocal spokesmen for their neighborhoods: some whose organizations HUD's earlier programs had funded; some which had grown from other federal programs; and others who now hoped to bring money to their neighborhoods.

Local elected officials saw the program as an opportunity to gain control of community development money for the first time and asserted their authority through bureaucratic reorganizations. But the program also stimulated enormous demands by the redevelopment agencies for continued funding, by other city agencies for new projects, and especially by neighborhood organizations for public-service projects. Elected officials could hope to satisfy only a few of the demands and decided instead to concentrate on a handful of key projects. The city agencies and neighborhood groups struggled among themselves for the remaining funds.

In both the "best cases," city officials fought against the intransigence of entrenched bureaucrats and sought to include citizen preferences in the design of the projects. In the "worst cases," the officials encountered delays from the overwhelming opposition of citizens and the intricate complexity of administrative arrangements. But despite the problems, local officials made substantial progress in implementing at least their pet projects—the "best cases." That is a conclusion their counterparts in the less-experienced cities envied.

NOTES

1. Allan R. Talbot, The Mayor's Game: Richard Lee of New Haven and the Politics of Change (New York: Praeger, 1970), p. 160.

2. Earl Selby, "New Haven: Where Federal Dollars Pay Off," Reader's Digest 94 (June 1969): 189-96. The literature on redevelopment in New Haven is voluminous. For a small sample, see Robert Dahl, Who Governs? Democracy and Power in an American City (New Haven: Yale University Press, 1961); Talbot, The Mayor's Game; Jeanne R. Lowe, "What Urban Renewal Can and Cannot Do," in Cities in a Race with Time (New York: Vintage Books, 1967), pp. 404-554; Fred Powledge, Model City (New York: Simon and Schuster, 1970); and Raymond Wolfinger, The Politics of Progress (Englewood Cliffs, N.J.: Prentice-Hall, 1973).

3. New Haven Journal Courier, March 16, 1976.

4. Letter from Mayor Frank Logue to Lawrence L. Thompson, Director of HUD's Hartford Area Office, May 13, 1976.

5. Ibid.

6. For an example of this argument, see Anthony Downs, "A Basic Perspective Concerning the Community Development Program," and "Using the Lessons of Experience to Allocate Resources in the Community Development Program," in Recommendations for Community Development Planning, ed. Anthony Downs, Lewis Bolan, and Margery al Chalabi (Chicago: Real Estate Research Corporation, 1975).

7. Press release, September 30, 1976.

8. News release, September 30, 1976.

9. New Haven Register, October 3, 1976.

10. Ibid.

11. News release, February 3, 1977.

12. Office of Neighborhood Preservation, "Monthly Report, June 1–July 1, 1977."

13. New Haven Redevelopment Agency, "Taft-Adams Housing Site Development Plan," January 16, 1975.

14. New Haven Register, March 2, 1975.

15. New Haven Register, April 7, 1977.

16. New Haven Register, April 8, 1977.

17. New Haven Advocate, April 13, 1977.

18. New London Day, December 11, 1975.

19. New London Day, January 29, 1976.

20. New London Day, January 28, 1977.

21. New London Day, February 1, 1977.

22. New London Day, August 19, 1976.

23. New London Day, February 12, 1976.

24. Statement by the President of the Southeastern Connecticut Chamber of Commerce, quoted in the New London Day, February 18, 1976.

25. New London Day, July 13, 1976.

26. New London Day, March 23, 1976.

27. New London Day, May 14, 1976.

28. Ibid.

29. Halcyon Limited, "Development and Marketing Program for the City of New London Central Business District," September 17, 1976.

30. Ibid.

31. New London Day, September 17, 1976.

32. New London Day, October 1, 1976.

33. New London Day, October 26, 1976.

34. New London Day, July 16, 1977.

35. New London Day, January 13, 1976.

36. New London Day, January 15, 1976.

37. New London Day, January 20, 1976.

38. New London Day, January 31, 1976.

39. Ibid.

40. New London Day, September 3, 1976.

41. New London Day, September 27, 1976.

4
BRIDGEPORT AND NORWICH

BRIDGEPORT

Connecticut's Industrial Leader

From 1890 to 1910, Bridgeport's population doubled to 100,000 residents as the city rapidly grew into one of New England's major manufacturing centers. By the middle of the century, the city was first in industrial production in Connecticut, the third in New England, and the ninth in the nation. As Bridgeport became more industrial, however, its suburbs grew into bedroom communities for New York. The city lost many of its wealthy citizens, the factories spread, the downtown stores aged, and the central business district deteriorated.

In 1970 city officials began an urban renewal project to replace old buildings with a new downtown shopping plaza. But this project, along with several others, still left large areas of vacant land and deteriorating housing in the city. Bridgeport also had a Model Cities program in a largely black and Hispanic East End neighborhood. Critics charged, though, that the program had done little for the city's poor.

Republican Mayor Nicholas Panuzio pledged to produce better results with the CDBG program. He established a new Office of Development Administration (ODA) in the fall of 1974 to fill two roles. First, he charged ODA with developing a comprehensive plan for the CDBG money. Second, he directed ODA to oversee the implementation of CDBG projects by other agencies in the city. The new office, he hoped, would bring federal community development money under city hall's unified control for the first time.

ODA's first director, Frank Williams, Jr., and his new staff had only a few months to prepare the city's first-year application for

its $4.1 million entitlement. Williams found that he had little dis-
cretion over half of the money. Bridgeport was legally committed
to completing its downtown renewal project and work scheduled for
the next year would take more than one-third of the entitlement.
Furthermore, he had to pay the cost of operating his own new agency
from CDBG money and that would cost another $400,000.

To determine how to allocate the other half of the entitlement
ODA's staff held a series of 11 meetings in the city's neighborhoods.
Some citizens suggested using the money for housing rehabilitation
but most residents favored neighborhood improvement projects—
better parks, more community centers, correction of flooding problems. Based on these suggestions and their own concepts, ODA's
staff members prepared a draft application. In addition to money
for the downtown renewal project and for ODA management, the application also included funding for housing rehabilitation, development of neighborhood parks (one of the cases we will explore shortly), and continuation of former Model Cities public service projects
(see Table 4.1). The Common Council, Bridgeport's city council,
quickly approved the application and Panuzio sent it off to HUD.

ODA then set out to formalize and broaden the citizen participation structure. It established a 50-member Citizens Union with
five members from each of the city's ten city council districts. The
citizens of each district would elect four of their representatives,
and the mayor would appoint the fifth. Forty of the members would
then separate into four functional task forces: parks and recreation,
public services, housing, and land use. The task forces would consider requests for projects, study the city's needs, and recommend
which projects should receive funding. The remaining ten members
would form the Citizens Council, an executive committee to review
the task force recommendations, hold hearings, and prepare final
recommendations for the city council.

After a tumultuous series of elections involving challenges
and charges of voting fraud, Bridgeport's neighborhoods finally
elected their citizen participation panel. The task forces began
holding hearings in the summer of 1975 and reviewing suggestions
for spending the city's $4.1 million second-year entitlement. In
November, the Union produced a five-page plan. They recommended
that the city continue most of its projects from the previous year,
but they also proposed a major new project: a $730,000 fund to ex-
pand the first year's park improvement project to every city neighborhood.

As the Citizens Union was deliberating, however, Panuzio resigned the mayoralty to take a job in the U.S. General Services Administration. Democrat John Mandanici went on to win the November
general election, and on taking office he reviewed the Citizens Union

recommendations. Mandanici set two new priorities. First, he wanted to improve the quality of housing in Bridgeport. Second, he wanted to improve the vitality of Bridgeport's downtown. To meet his first goal, he ordered more than half of the money earmarked for the Citizen Union's park improvement project to housing rehabilitation. For the second goal, he reserved $100,000 for redevelopment of the city's waterfront (another of the cases). The Union angrily protested but the city council, all Democrats, sided with the mayor. The resulting application increased the money for redevelopment, rehabilitation, public services, and administration and decreased the allocation for parks.

TABLE 4.1

Bridgeport: Allocation of Money by Function
(in percentages)

| Function | Year* | | | Total |
	I (1975)	II (1976)	III (1977)	
Downtown renewal	0	2	4	2
Municipal services and equipment	0	0	0	0
Urban renewal	35	35	35	35
Housing rehabilitation	16	17	11	15
Neighborhood parks and facilities	25	11	12	16
Neighborhood public works	0	1	1	1
Social services	11	17	17	15
Planning and administration	13	9	15	12
Other	0	8	4	4
Total	100	100	100	100
Amount (in millions of dollars)	$4.1	$4.1	$3.8	$12.0

*For local program year ending in calendar year shown.
Source: Derived from proposed activities in local applications.

As the Citizens Union began deliberating their third-year recommendations a few months later, they faced serious organizational problems. The Union had a large number of new members who needed schooling in the intricacies of the CDBG program and many older members who attended only sporadically. Mandanici's quarrel with the Union, furthermore, left many Union members uncertain about whether the new administration would take their recommendations seriously. The Union also questioned whether ODA was producing results. One Union member complained that "with the exception of a few social services programs we have accomplished nothing."[1]

Despite the wrangling, the Union's recommendations for the city's third-year entitlement was almost identical to the ODA's proposals. The two groups disagreed over a few individual projects, such as a $26,000 dental-care project, a $20,000 downtown tree-planting project, and the ODA budget, but even these differences angered the Union. They charged that the mayor was manipulating the application without consulting them. City officials replied that they had given the Union every opportunity to be heard.

Mandanici pressed his own program before the city council, and the council gave their approval. Compared with the first two years, the differences in the $3.8 million third-year application were relatively minor—less money for housing rehabilitation, more money for more public-service projects. The minor changes, however, masked growing strife between the Citizens Union and the city administration.

Best Case: Park Improvement Project

Despite Bridgeport's nickname, "The Park City," some neighborhoods had retained little open space as the city grew. In planning the first-year application, ODA officials decided the city should use some of its CDBG money to improve neighborhood parks, and they earmarked $405,000 for the project. Because of the time pressures for submitting the application, however, they did not consult extensively with the planners at the park department who would implement the project. In fact, they had not even determined which park projects the city would undertake with the money.

After the city obtained HUD's approval for the application, the park department began planning how to spend the money it had received. The department had complete plans on file for two proposed facilities: the construction of tennis courts in an existing park in the city's relatively affluent North End and the reclamation of a dumping ground underneath an elevated section of the Connecticut Turnpike in the lower-income South End of the city. Earlier, the plans had been stalled for lack of money. Now, with CDBG funds providing the $113,000 needed for the two projects, the park department began work.

That left the park department with nearly $300,000 remaining to allocate. A department planner referred to an earlier inventory of Bridgeport's park needs and formulated plans for four other projects: a neighborhood playground in the relatively poor East End; a softball field in the North End; a park in the central business district; and a park along the waterfront. The park department also planned to use the CDBG funds to match grant funds from the U.S. Bureau of Outdoor Recreation's* Land and Water Conservation Fund (administered in Connecticut by the State Department of Environmental Protection). The fund enabled states to make grants for the development of publicly owned space, especially in urban areas. By using CDBG funds as the required local match, the park department could double the amount of money available to improve local parks.

First, however, the city charter required the department to obtain the approval of its oversight body, the park board. Some members of the board opposed the East End neighborhood playground but strongly supported the park in the central business district. To win passage of all the proposals, the park department packaged the four parks into a single "project" and the board members gave their approval. But the long process, first developing the plans, then securing needed approval from the park board, and finally preparing the environmental reviews required for all CDBG projects, delayed the start of construction on the projects. By the end of 1975, half-way through the first program year, Bridgeport had spent no money on the park projects.

When construction finally did begin on the softball field in the North End in early 1976, neighborhood residents angrily protested the plans. The softball field, some neighbors complained, would bring noise, congestion, and possible "undesirables" into the area. One ODA staff member was more blunt: "They are afraid of minority people . . . coming into their neighborhood. They want the open space, but they don't want it developed."

The park department had not met with the citizens before beginning construction on the park, and the protests now forced them to hold a series of meetings to gauge local sentiment. Testimony at the hearings overwhelmingly opposed development of park land near homes, so the park board voted to construct instead two new tennis courts adjacent to some existing courts in a remote area of the park. This decision drew still more complaints, this time about building tennis courts in an affluent part of town, but the park board decided to continue construction. And henceforth, the board concluded, it would hold public hearings before beginning work on new projects.

---

*The Bureau is part of the U.S. Department of the Interior.

Meanwhile, the newly formed Citizens Union began meeting to set its priorities for funding during the second year of the program. The Union's Open Space and Community Facilities Task Force worked with ODA's parks planner and held a series of public hearings to gather suggestions. The task force emerged with a recommendation for $730,600 for improvements to 19 neighborhood parks and after considering the recommendations of the other task forces, the Citizens Union as a whole concurred.

The proposed improvements covered every part of the city. "The citizens owed a degree of allegiance to the area they represented," one ODA staff member explained. Another added that there was a tendency to "give everybody a piece of something." The proposed park improvements gave every member of the Union a portion of the CDBG allocation for his or her own district. It was one way, members thought, to make sure that all areas of the city benefited from the CDBG program.

After Mayor John Mandanici took office in January he began a review of the second-year recommendations for funding with his new ODA director, Robert Testo. The only major change Mandanici ordered was a cut of over $400,000 from the $730,600 park improvement budget proposed by the Union. He transferred $300,000 of the money to the Park City Housing Development Corporation for its housing rehabilitation and allocated the remaining $100,000 to the Youth Outreach and Prevention Program, a public-service project to reduce juvenile delinquency in the western and northern ends of the city. The Park Department, he said, could make up the $400,000 from its own funds.*

Members of the Union were angry. At a hearing before the city council, Nancy Altieri, chairperson of the Citizens Union, charged that the mayor's action destroyed the Union's recommendations. Other members of the Union called the decision a travesty and a sham. The city council, however, supported the mayor by reducing the park improvements allocation to $330,000 and requiring the park board to match the CDBG funds from its own resources. This combination of funds provided money for all of the park projects at a reduced rate, but the decision left the members of the Citizens Union angry.

The park department began work on the second-year projects in July 1976. Unlike the first year, the second-year application

---

*Several years earlier, the park department had received a settlement from the state for the acquisition of city park land for a new highway. The department set aside the money as a trust fund for park development.

listed each of the parks which were to receive CDBG funds. The contractors ordered the needed materials, but by the time the supplies arrived the weather was too cold to begin construction. As the weather improved in the spring of 1977 the department finally could complete the projects.

The second-year allocation ended the city's major commitment to park improvements. After meeting with Mandanici, ODA planners decided that the city should allocate only $80,000 for parks in the third year of the CDBG program and that the money should be reserved for expected cost overruns on the second-year projects. ODA staff reported its recommendations to the Open Space and Community Facilities Task Force and, after considering ODA's arguments that the available CDBG funds would not permit further expansion of the park projects, the task force reluctantly agreed. Later, the Citizens Union and the city council concurred.

Worst Case: Waterfront Park Project

Just a few blocks from Bridgeport's downtown the city's once scenic Pequonnock River waterfront had become an eyesore. The riverside property had fostered the growth of Bridgeport's industry, but by the early 1970s abandoned factories, petroleum tank farms, and junk yards cluttered the land. The scene presented visitors to the city with an unsightly panorama and created a negative image of the downtown area for city residents.

City officials had struggled with the problem for years. Since 1970 the Redevelopment Agency had been working on nearby Congress Plaza, an $8 million federal urban renewal project to clear old buildings and bring new housing and commercial facilities to the central business district, but the project had created little more than a few boarded-up buildings and acres of vacant land near the waterfront. A sign hanging on a closed movie theater proclaimed: "You are looking at the center of Congress Plaza. Hopes have grown from promises made by City Hall in 1971. Is this the spirit in which City Hall keeps all of its promises? Don't hold your breath to find out—this building is still waiting. . . ."

A few blocks away, however, a group of promoters had begun construction on a new jai alai fronton on the site of a vacant truck assembly plant along one bank of the Pequonnock. The new facility would offer a restaurant, sport, and betting, a combination that promised to bring Bridgeport both new visitors and added tax revenue. As ODA planners in 1975 considered projects for second-year funding, they suggested that CDBG funds could be used to develop the opposite bank of the river and thus bring new vitality to the city's downtown. Although ODA had no specific proposals for the project, the Citizens Union agreed on the value of doing something for the area and concurred on a $100,000 allocation.

John Mandanici took office a few months later and seized the Waterfront Park concept as the centerpiece of his CDBG program. Bridgeport, he told HUD, would use the $100,000 for "modest" and "cosmetic" activities along the waterfront "with the goal of improving the area's attractiveness."[2] However, he had not yet developed a firm idea of what Bridgeport should do with the money.

ODA planners reviewed a collection of earlier proposals for the land, including marinas, parks, and other recreational facilities, to gather ideas for the project and by early June the outline of the project emerged. The Waterfront Park, the planners said, should serve a dual purpose: developing the waterfront as a recreational resource to improve its commercial potential. The city would replace the vacant tract with:

- a pier to provide a promenade for walking and fishing;
- benches and improved lighting to encourage people to sit by the river;
- a bikeway to become part of a proposed system of bikeways throughout the city;
- improvements to an existing dock;
- a transient marina to accommodate 30 boats; and
- improved access roads to the park from downtown. (Elevated railroad tracks effectively isolated the site from the rest of the city.)

City officials viewed the proposal as the cornerstone of a comprehensive strategy to bring economic vitality back to downtown Bridgeport. The jai alai fronton would bring people into the area. The Waterfront Park, they hoped, would convince them to spend more time downtown once they got there. The mayor also hoped that the Waterfront Park would anchor even more ambitious plans, including conversion of the city's nearby former railroad station into a specialty food mart and transformation of a retired ferryboat into a riverside seafood restaurant.

The Citizens Union had approved a broad concept for the site but they angrily opposed ODA's plans. The project, they said, was a job for private enterprise, not for CDBG funds. Furthermore, ODA had announced the plans without meeting with the group to obtain their approval and the Union accused the agency of attempting to "push the project down our throats" and of "underhandedness."[3] ODA also appeared to be moving quickly on the Waterfront Project while construction on one of the Union's favorite projects, a neighborhood center for the city's East End, moved with painful slowness.

The Union adopted a resolution opposing the project and wrote to HUD to urge the agency to review the plans. Not only was the proposed Waterfront Park not a fit use for public funds, they complained, but the use of the funds for a marina was ineligible under HUD's rules. HUD investigated and discovered that Bridgeport had moved considerably beyond the earlier sketchy plans for "modest" and "cosmetic" improvements. The city could not spend CDBG funds for the marina, HUD ruled, because the marina was essentially a transit terminal and transit terminals were an ineligible use of CDBG funds.

John Hyslop, ODA's planning director, understood the Citizen Union's anger at not being consulted before the city announced its plans. He explained, however, that he had discovered that the proposed Waterfront Park project was eligible for funding by the Federal Bureau of Outdoor Recreation's Land and Water Conservation Fund. The city planned to use $230,000 in CDBG funds (the second-year allocation plus additional funds in the third year) as the required local match for $280,000 from the Bureau of Outdoor Recreation. But to be eligible for the funds, ODA had to prepare the application and rush it to the Connecticut Department of Environmental Protection, which administered the money in the state. There was no time to consult with the citizens, Hyslop said. But the rush combined with Mandanici's earlier reversal of the Union's recommendations for parks projects and the slow pace of construction on the neighborhood facility to damage seriously the relations between ODA and the Citizens Union.

By the time the Union's letter reached HUD, however, city officials had already halted planning for the marina. Workers had discovered two old barges under water at the site, and the State Historic Preservation Commission reported that they were of the type that once plied the Erie Canal. The barges had great historical value, the commission told city officials, and the city should not destroy them. The city solicited bids for raising the barges intact and discovered it would cost $105,000, more than the city believed its CDBG budget could bear. The Federal Bureau of Outdoor Recreation might fund the recovery of the barges, ODA officials learned, but approval had to come from Washington. They feared this would entail even more delays, and they decided to drop the marina from the project just as HUD ruled it ineligible.

As ODA staff members discussed the revised proposal with state officials in Hartford, they also discovered that Bridgeport did not own the land on which the city proposed to build the park and that the Bureau of Outdoor Recreation funded projects only on publicly owned land. ODA officials conducted a title search and found that some of the land belonged to Consolidated Rail Corporation, which leased it to the State Department of Transportation for its commuter rail service, which subleased it to the city. The local privately owned electric company owned another plot, and the city owned the remainder.

The city eventually acquired title to all the land in the project area and filed a revised application with the Connecticut Department of Environmental Protection in the spring of 1977. City officials hoped to use CDBG funds to start construction on the project while awaiting a decision on their application. Not only were they anxious to begin work on the project they had announced more than a year earlier with such high expectations, but they also hoped that a start on the project would favorably influence the decision on the city's application for Bureau of Outdoor Recreation funds.

Bridgeport officials also learned they needed a series of permits before they could begin construction. Because the project involved an inland waterway, the city needed a permit from the State Department of Environmental Protection. Because the project involved a navigable waterway, the city also needed several permits from the U.S. Army Corps of Engineers. First the barge problem and later a series of technical questions about the details of the project delayed the permits. Finally, late in the spring of 1977, the city obtained the necessary approvals and began removing old pilings from the river.

By autumn, the city had spent $46,000 on removing the pilings but still had not received formal notification of the status of its application for federal Bureau of Outdoor Recreation funds. The project was dormant awaiting the decision. ODA officials confidently expected to receive official approval of their application by Thanksgiving and planned to begin construction on the project early in 1978. But two years after discussions about the project began, the Waterfront Park was still no more than a plan.

NORWICH

Once a Mill Town

Until the early twentieth century, Norwich was a thriving textile mill town. Built along the city's twin rivers, the mills gave Norwich a strong economy and sustained growth. In the first half of the twentieth century, however, the mills gradually joined the exodus of other New England industries to the South. Norwich was a single-industry town, and the mill closings brought hardship.

But despite the availability of federal urban renewal funds to rebuild the town, Norwich conducted only two large redevelopment projects. In the early 1960s the city spent $1.2 million to clear a group of old downtown commercial buildings. Then in 1973 Norwich began a $7 million project to remove deteriorating houses on a bluff overlooking the central business district. As the CDBG program began in the fall of 1974, that tract remained vacant.

To administer the city's $1.5 million annual entitlement, the city council instructed City Manager Charles Whitty to establish a small four-member Office of Community Development. The council had considered using the staff of the Redevelopment Agency but as one council member explained, "The Council wanted greater control over the program. The feeling on the Council was that the Redevelopment Agency was not as responsive [to the Council] as it could be."

The council also resurrected a seven-member citizen group, the Community Development Action Plan Agency, that had been part of a statewide community development planning program in the late 1960s. The council charged the agency with surveying citizen opinions on the use of the funds and, during the first year of the program, the group held more than 15 meetings and collected more than 50 suggestions from citizens for projects. Attendance at the agency's meetings, however, was small—fewer than 20 citizens testified at the first hearing. The citizens overwhelmingly favored projects to improve their neighborhoods: resurfacing streets, constructing new sidewalks, clearing deteriorating houses. Several city agencies also requested funds; the largest request was from the Redevelopment Agency for twice the city's entitlement.

The citizen group worked closely with Whitty and followed his guidance in narrowing the projects to a few recommendations: continuation of the city's redevelopment project (to which the city was legally committed); renewal of an area near an historic waterfall (one of the case studies for Norwich); and blight removal in an unspecified area (the second case).

Several council members favored using the "blight clearance" money to prepare a site for a new downtown housing project for the elderly. One citizen countered that this and other proposed projects were too "downtown oriented" and suggested the city use the money instead to extend municipal water and sewer services.[4] The council members rejected that proposal, but they were unsure of precisely what they did want to do with the money. They decided finally to follow the citizen group's general recommendations. The council earmarked two-thirds of the money for renewal projects and another one-fifth for public works (see Table 4.2). But they reserved decisions on which specific projects would receive funding.

When the city council began deliberations for the second-year application they decided to disband the citizens group and hold their own hearings. The council not only "wanted to get involved," one council member explained, but "the council wanted to assert its control over the program." The council's public hearings produced more requests for neighborhood public works, particularly for extending the city water system to several neighborhoods that did not have municipal service.

TABLE 4.2

Norwich: Allocation of Money by Function
(in percentages)

| | Year* | | | |
| | I | II | III | |
Function	(1975)	(1976)	(1977)	Total
Downtown renewal	0	0	0	0
Municipal services and equipment	7	0	(b)	2
Urban renewal	65	68	26	53
Housing rehabilitation	12	24	0	12
Neighborhood parks and facilities	0	0	5	2
Neighborhood public works	15	0	44	20
Social services	0	0	10	3
Planning and administration	1	2	5	3
Other	0	6	10	5
Total	100	100	100	100
Amount (in millions of dollars)	$1.5	$1.5	$1.5	$4.4[c]

[a]For local program year ending in calendar year shown.
[b]Less than 0.5 percent.
[c]Total does not add due to rounding.
Source: Derived from proposed activities in local applications.

Whitty recommended that the city use its second-year entitlement to extend the water system, to continue the redevelopment projects begun in the first year, and to use some CDBG money as the required local match for a state grant to purchase the Norwich Golf Course. The water project dominated the council debate, and many council members feared that the eventual cost of the project would be too high. The council finally followed its first-year course: it allocated most of the money for the redevelopment projects and (instead of public works) the golf course. But the council left decisions on specific projects until later.

Several public service agencies showed special interest in the CDBG money as the council members took up the third-year application in the fall of 1976. Speakers for public-service projects made special appeals and the council decided to fund five of them. The council allotted most of the rest of the money to completing the city's urban renewal project and to continuing a group of public-works projects begun during the first year.

The third-year application looked far different from the first two. Nearly half of the money went for public works (compared with only one-fifth during the first year) and only one-quarter went for redevelopment (compared with two-thirds during the first two years). The new dominance of public works was a result of the troubles the first-year renewal projects had encountered (as we shall see shortly). Norwich had spent almost none of its first two years' entitlement. In the third year, the council gave money to the public works department for a group of small-scale projects. The council knew these projects were feasible and the money would be spent.

Best Case: Falls Project

In 1643, a force of Narragansett Indians marched on a band of Mohegans camped around what is now Norwich. Uncas, leader of the Mohegans, rallied his braves and trapped the Narragansett tribe along a cliff overlooking a waterfall. Faced with a choice between death at the hands of the Mohegans and a chance of surviving the plunge over the falls, the Narragansetts chose the falls. Many of them died in the leap, but their leader escaped, only to be captured later by the British and turned over to Uncas for execution.

The story of Uncas' cleverness became a popular local legend, and Norwich's first settlers preserved the picturesque Falls area. As the city grew, one of the city's mills acquired the property. The company built a large complex just below the Falls area, built the neighborhood into a thriving community, but kept the Falls as park land. The mill moved South in the middle of the twentieth century, however, and the buildings gradually fell into disrepair. Several of the mill houses nearby deteriorated as well, although many of them still served as homes for Norwich's poor.

During discussion over the use of the first year CDBG funds, several citizens—including one council member who grew up in the neighborhood—suggested that the city use some of the money to do something to improve the Falls area. The area was a "pocket of blight," the citizens argued, within a neighborhood that was attracting a growing number of professional offices. The area was small and the citizens believed the city could make substantial improve-

ments within the resources of Norwich's $1.5 million CDBG entitle-
ment. The CDAP Agency, City Manager Whitty, and the city council all agreed, so the city allotted $400,000 for a project in the first-
year application. The amount of money, however, was no more than
a consensus that it would be a good idea to devote a large share of
the city's entitlement to the project. "By the time the application
went in," one city official explained, the city was not "sure of the
scope or cost of the project."

After HUD approved the application, city officials began dis-
cussing what to do with the money. Three concepts emerged. First,
city officials agreed that they should use some of the money to improve a road that ran past the Falls to the old mill. There was a
sharp, sloped curve on the road that made passage difficult in the
winter snow. If the area was to be improved, city officials concluded, the road would have to be straightened.

Second, the owner of the old mill had donated several acres of
land around the Falls to the city several years before. Development
of the property into a city park, the officials thought, would improve
the ambiance of the neighborhood.

Finally, the old mill houses in the neighborhood had deteriorated badly. At first, Whitty and the council considered total clearance of the houses to prepare the land for more offices or perhaps
an apartment complex. The costs, however, proved far higher than
the city's CDBG resources. "It was obvious very quickly," Whitty
explained, "that that was going to mean big bucks. You couldn't
justify it in terms of what the return would be in taxes." Instead
the officials trimmed their plans to clearance of the worst houses
and rehabilitation of the remaining dwellings. This, they hoped,
would make property available to adjoining landowners with small
lots and would encourage them to improve their own buildings.

The three elements of the plan—road reconstruction, park development, and selective acquisition and demolition of the houses—
would cost $1.2 million, city planners estimated. During delibera-
tions for the city's second-year funds, the council added another
$305,000 to the $400,000 from the first year and tentatively earmarked the balance from the city's expected third-year entitlement.

In December 1975, however, all planning for the Falls project
stopped. During a conversation with an official from the Connecticut
State Historic Preservation Commission about a different matter, a
city administrator discovered that the entire Falls area was listed
on the National Register of Historic Places.

Three years earlier, the Society of the Founders of Norwich,
the local historical society, had petitioned the state commission to
have the area placed on the register. The old mill houses, they said,
were fine representations of nineteenth-century mill life. The federal

government had approved the designation, a step that not only carried prestige but also required that all agencies using federal funds—including CDBG—for projects involving sites on the register make every effort possible to avoid destruction of historic property.

The discovery that the area was a nationally designated historic district amazed city officials. The federal government had not notified the city of the action* and "We never even considered the idea these buildings might be landmarks," Whitty explained.[5] Another administrator added, "I see no value in those [houses] at all." The city hired architects to examine the buildings in more detail and learned that some of the structures had been built more than one hundred years before as temporary shelters. The buildings had neither foundations nor cellars and, the architects said, were never meant to last.

Nevertheless, the state commission advised the Federal Advisory Council on Historic Preservation of the city's plans and in March 1976 the city received a formal order from the advisory council to stop all work on the project pending a council investigation. A member of the federal council's staff visited the Falls area with a staff member from the state commission and concluded that the city's plans, if allowed to continue, would destroy important historic resources. Norwich, the federal officials said, should save all of the houses.

Saving all of the houses, Norwich officials countered, would make the city's primary goal—widening the road and straightening the curve—impossible. The advisory council suggested an alternative. The city could move the houses back from the road. Then, they said, Norwich could improve the road and rehabilitate the houses.

The Office of Community Development spent the autumn of 1976 investigating these suggestions. After consulting with several engineers, however, they discovered that it would cost $275,000 to move the houses, a cost that would nearly drain the city's first-year allocation for the project before any work on the city's three-part project could begin. Furthermore, the engineers warned that the move might not be successful. Some of the buildings were large, all were old, and none had basements. Whitty wrote the advisory council and contended that " moving those buildings back from the

_____

*The Federal Register, however, annually publishes a complete list of sites on the National Register of Historic Places. The Falls area's status as an historic district was thus a matter of public record.

road to facilitate widening is too costly and impractical to be considered a feasible alternative."[6] And, he added, the city could not "justify the expenditure of over $200,000 to move and rehabilitate the . . . houses when there is no assurance that anyone will acquire the rehabilitated buildings."[7]

The federal officials did not want to sacrifice any of the houses to the city's plans. The city, on the other hand, wanted to improve the road, develop the park, and remove at least some of the worst of the houses. City officials ironically reminded themselves that had they chosen to pursue the project with local instead of CDBG funds, the Federal Advisory Council would have been powerless to interfere.

The continued delays frustrated city officials and in March 1977 City Manager Whitty wrote an angry letter to the Federal Advisory Council:

> We are frankly extremely disturbed with the amount of time we have devoted in the past two (2) years in complying with Advisory Council procedures and with the lack of progress in resolving historic concerns. . . . [W]ithout question, we have been most severely frustrated in our efforts to implement our CD programs as a result of the extremely lengthy and time-consuming procedures we have encountered in our effort to comply with [federal historic preservation guidelines]. . . .
>
> It seems unreasonable to demand that such disproportionate amounts of time and money be spent on preserving every historic structure in Norwich, despite conditions or circumstances. Further, the people who live in the Falls area have lost faith in the City because they cannot understand the seemingly endless delays in revitalizing their neighborhood.[8]

Whitty attached to the letter a five-page record of the city's attempts to begin work on the Falls project to document his frustration.

By early summer, the city and the Federal Advisory Commission reached agreement on a three-phase division of work on the project. The city would begin with the least controversial portion, creating a park around the Falls. Then the city would improve the street, although the city would not widen the road because of the cost of moving the houses. Finally, the city would rehabilitate—within Federal Advisory Council guidelines—as many of the old homes as possible and would not demolish any of the buildings without the concurrence of the Connecticut State Commission and the Federal Advisory Council.

The city hired an engineer to prepare the park improvement plans and hoped to begin work on the Falls project in the spring of 1978, more than three years after the Norwich City Council first approved funds for the project. "It's been such an incredible experience dealing with the federal officials in this matter," Whitty said. "It has delayed the project far beyond what we thought it would." The whole process, Whitty said,

> has been frustrating to us. The city of Norwich has an excellent record in historic preservation. It's not a case where the city has no interest in its historic past. But the city also has current needs and the problem is where the two come into conflict. . . .
> I'm convinced that what might come from this is that future efforts will be made to avoid getting involved in historic situations.

The result, Whitty concluded, was that the city ended up "spending money to justify what [it was] doing instead of doing it."

Worst Case: Rose Tower Project

Downtown Norwich in 1975 looked nearly the same as when the mills closed—except for the deterioration that the years had brought. The stores gradually lost customers to outlying shopping malls and the area lost much of its vitality and many of its residents. To reverse the area's decline, the Norwich Community Development Corporation—a local citizens agency established under state charter to help improve the community—solicited proposals from developers for a major housing project for the elderly.*

One proposal emerged in January 1975. Norman Shapiro, a Hartford-based developer involved in several other Norwich projects, presented plans for a seven-story tower with shops on the bottom floor. Shapiro's proposal impressed council members but, a city official recalled, "it was just a germ of an idea." The council decided to set aside $768,000 in the first-year entitlement—the estimated site preparation costs. But because there were no firm

---

*The Norwich Community Development Corporation was similar to the New Haven Development Corporation, the agency involved in New Haven's Taft Project. It had no connection with the Community Development Action Plan Agency.

plans, the council budgeted the amount as a "blight clearance" project in an unspecified area.

Shapiro and his associates prepared complete plans for the project over the next few months and in the early fall of 1975 they made a lengthy presentation to the council. The council held closed discussions with Shapiro during the next few meetings and finally, in December, the full details of the $2 million project emerged. For the construction of "Rose Tower," as the project had been named, the council would use the "blight clearance" money to acquire the property on a downtown block, relocate the occupants, demolish the buildings, and prepare the site for construction. The city would then transfer the site to Shapiro, either through a gift, sale, or long-term lease. Meanwhile, Shapiro would apply to HUD for $194,000 in Section 8 subsidies and to the Federal Housing Administration for mortgage insurance. Shapiro would then build a four-story 50-unit apartment complex for the elderly (instead of the larger building discussed earlier) that would also include a parking garage, several stores, and a drive-in bank.

The plans attracted the support of many local citizens. An official of the Norwich Chamber of Commerce announced his support and City Manager Whitty said that the development would increase the city's annual tax yield on the property from $25,000 to $75,000. Members of the Norwich Community Development Corporation agreed with several members of the city council that the project would help stimulate new growth in the downtown area.

But the plans also drew opposition. City council member Walter Way called Rose Tower "a bum deal for Norwich" and added, "I think the taxpayers of our community will be up in arms when they realize what is going on." Way questioned "the philosophy of using community development money to assist private interests." He condemned the lack of competitive bidding for the project and suggested that "vested interests" were involved "in a Watergate-type operation" to "hand the land over to a private developer—scot free." The result, he said, was that "the Shapiro plan is not a Rose Tower for the City and its taxpayers. It is a Rose Folly if ever I saw one."[9]

Council President Konstant Morrell contended in January 1976 that the majority of council members favored the project. Way nevertheless maintained his opposition, saying, "The true intent of this [CDBG] funding was to help poor people and that's not going to happen with the plan before us."[10] But despite Way's opposition, the council at the end of January gave an 8-1 vote of confidence in requesting the Norwich Community Development Corporation to continue its negotiations for the acquisition of property for the project. The vote, however, did not give the council's formal approval for the project and Whitty warned the council that they had to take some action quickly.

A short time later another council member joined Way in opposition to the project and the two council members discussed seeking a citywide referendum to test voter sentiment on the Rose Tower proposal. The Taxpayers Association of Norwich added their "vigorous opposition" to using CDBG money to prepare the site for a private developer and then selling it to him for such a low price.[11] Council President Morrell still expressed his confidence that he could muster the votes for the proposal, but support for Rose Tower continued to crumble as a third council member joined the opposition.

In the face of growing opposition, the Norwich Community Development Corporation withdrew from its supporting and mediating roles. The objections of the three council members, the corporation said, had effectively killed the project. A letter from the corporation to Council President Morrell explained: "To date the [Norwich Community Development Corporation] has not been engaged in any public controversy and it is our opinion that we should not be involved in a public controversy regarding the Rose Tower project."[12]

The Norwich Bulletin editorially concluded sadly that "the controversial Rose Tower project for downtown Norwich seems to be dead." The newspaper added, "It is, we suppose, not complimentary either to the NCDC [Norwich Community Development Corporation] or the Council to say that they have panicked—less because there is opposition than because there is uncertainty in the minds of many citizens about the merits of the Rose Tower proposal."[13] The death of the proposal, the paper warned, might mean "the start of a general exodus from downtown" that would "spell the finish to downtown Norwich."[14]

But supporters of the project did not surrender and council member Raymond Botti announced he would make "one last try" to save the project. "I think it is necessary for the downtown area, we have the money, and it is a legitimate use of the funds," he argued.[15] A public hearing called to discuss Botti's proposal, however, drew a large crowd and the citizens opposed the plan by a margin of seven to one.

In early March, the council went through a complex series of parliamentary battles as opponents tried to scuttle the project and supporters struggled to keep it alive. The opposition was strong but observers speculated that the council could still muster a majority in favor of Rose Tower. But the council decided to table the question for a month until they saw revised plans from Shapiro.

Meanwhile, Shapiro's application to HUD for Section 8 subsidies had encountered problems. HUD's environmental studies revealed that the project site, bordering on several major downtown streets, had traffic noise too loud for occupants in the proposed tower. Unless Shapiro could demonstrate that he could effectively insulate the apartments, HUD told him, the agency would reject his application. Shapiro told city officials that he was still interested in the project and was confident he could solve the noise problem. But members of the city council now told him that they wanted to change the terms of transferring the property from a one dollar sale to either a fair market value sale or a long-term lease.

As the council prepared to meet with Shapiro on April 1, 1976, to discuss the two new problems, HUD notified the city that it had rejected Shapiro's request for Section 8 subsidies because of the noise problems. Shapiro had awaited a commitment from the council before undertaking the cost of new engineering studies for the project. When the council delayed, Shapiro abandoned Rose Tower and obtained HUD approval for an alternative Section 8 housing proposal in the city's outskirts. "I don't think the city was committed to solving the problems," one city official explained, and the noise pollution question "gave those who felt boxed in a chance to escape." Meanwhile, several downtown merchants were watching the outcome of the Rose Tower project as a measure of the city's commitment to the central business district. When the project failed, they moved their shops—as the Bulletin had feared—to new shopping malls in the city's outlying areas.

The collapse of the Rose Tower project left half of the city's first-year entitlement unallocated at the end of the program year. The council finally decided in the fall of 1976 to spend the money instead on a new downtown parking garage and a series of street improvement projects. HUD approved the city's amended application in April 1977, and Norwich prepared to begin many of its "first-year" projects—two years late.

CONCLUSION

Bridgeport and Norwich had fewer and less powerfully entrenched interests than the more experienced cities. Neighborhood organizations, where they existed at all, were far weaker. Citizen demands were relatively modest and centered on neighborhood improvements—more parks, better streets, expanded water service. The redevelopment agencies were relatively smaller and had fewer ongoing projects. The two cities consequently had less political conflict. Local elected officials, furthermore, had less difficulty in controlling the program and asserting their own demands for projects to improve the appearance, vitality, and economic strength of the downtown areas.

Despite the lower level of conflict, however, the less experienced cities had substantially more difficulty in implementing their projects. Norwich's "best case" was best only in that it offered city officials hope for eventual progress. The projects most important to elected officials in both cities were ironically also the "worst case" projects. Citizen opposition, the complexity of the projects, and an inability to plan solutions to problems crippled some of the most important projects in the less experienced cities.

The next two chapters will examine these issues in more detail. Chapter 5 will explore the issues of planning, budgeting, and controlling the program. Chapter 6 will probe the factors that contributed to successes and failures in the execution of the projects.

NOTES

1. Bridgeport Telegram, January 25, 1977.
2. City of Bridgeport, "Application for Federal Assistance," [CDBG application to HUD], January 6, 1974.
3. Bridgeport Post, July 1, 1976.
4. Norwich Bulletin, November 26, 1974.
5. Norwich Bulletin, December 29, 1975.
6. Letter from Charles Whitty to Jordan Tannebaum of the Federal Advisory Council on Historic Preservation, December 12, 1976.
7. Ibid.
8. Letter from Charles Whitty to John D. McDermott of the Federal Advisory Council on Historic Preservation, March 22, 1977.
9. Norwich Bulletin, December 16, 1975.
10. Norwich Bulletin, January 13, 1976.
11. Norwich Bulletin, February 11, 1976.
12. Quoted in the Norwich Bulletin, February 14, 1976.
13. Norwich Bulletin, February 16, 1977.
14. Ibid.
15. Norwich Bulletin, February 16, 1976.

5
BUDGETING THE MONEY

SHIFTS IN AUTHORITY

Decentralization of Power to the Cities

Whatever else might have resulted from the CDBG program, it clearly shifted power over community development policy to the cities. Far more than in the categorical programs, the cities could determine, relatively free from federal control, which local projects should receive federal aid. As Nixon promised in 1971, power and resources truly did flow back to the cities from the federal government. HUD reviews centered on procedural issues such as the adequacy of the required housing assistance plan and local compliance with the many piggyback federal requirements such as equal employment opportunity and review of the projects' environmental impact. The cities had broad discretion over the substance of local development projects. "At all times, " a HUD area office official reported, "the sense of responsibility of achievement rests with the local chief executive officer and not with us. "

The transfer of authority was not total. HUD area office officials sometimes haggled extensively with local officials over the eligibility of proposed projects. HUD officials also dispensed a great deal of technical assistance which ranged from answers to questions on the eligibility of projects to advice on how to fill out

---

Portions of this chapter originally appeared as "Can the Cities Be Trusted? The Community Development Experience. " Reprinted with permission from the Political Science Quarterly 94 (Fall 1979): 437-51.

the application forms. Furthermore, as we saw in Chapter 2, both Congress and HUD gradually drew back some of the discretion originally delegated to the cities. But on the whole the CDBG program indisputably increased local discretion in using federal money for local development projects.

Centralization of Power to City Hall

Within the cities, local elected officials used the program's authority to bring community development policy under central control. Unlike the earlier categorical grants that went to relatively independent redevelopment or Model Cities agencies, the CDBG program gave responsibility for the money directly to each community's chief executive officer. In Bridgeport and New Haven (with mayor-council governments), the chief elected official was the mayor; in New London and Norwich (with council-manager governments), the chief elected officials were the city council members. But although the formal positions of the officials varied by city, their goal did not: to concentrate control over the money in their own hands.

The first strategy that these officials developed was administrative reorganization designed both to weaken the redevelopment agencies and to centralize control over the money. The less experienced cities—Bridgeport and Norwich—established new bureaus to plan and execute the program. Officials in the more experienced cities—New Haven and New London—could not have so outflanked their more powerful redevelopment agencies. They furthermore realized that they would have to rely on the expertise of the agencies to implement the projects. Both cities did, however, establish "mini-bureaus" close to elected officials to supervise the work of the redevelopment agencies and other administrative agencies. New London established a formal Office of Community Development. New Haven relied on an informal committee of the mayor's closest advisers.

The reorganizations in all four cities served as much symbolic as administrative purposes. The mayors and the council members wanted to relay clearly a message to the citizens and particularly to the redevelopment agencies: the act gave elected officials control over the program and they intended to exercise it.

HOW DID THE CITIES DECIDE ?

After strengthening their control over the use of the funds, local elected officials set out to budget the money. Although the details of the process varied by city, each city went through three identifiable phases in allocating its CDBG funds: setting the decision-making agenda; narrowing the choices; and hearing the appeals.

Setting the Agenda

The executive—mayor or city-manager—asked city agencies to propose ideas for funding, and the agencies returned with long "shopping lists." They proposed ideas which had rested on a planner's shelf for years, projects which had been denied funding from other sources, or in the case of the redevelopment agencies, large-scale projects for which CDBG was the only source of funds. The New London Public Works Department, for example, proposed to improve the city's water system with a new $8 million reservoir. New Haven's Redevelopment Agency listed $150 million in uncompleted projects, for which it needed CDBG funds. The projects proposed by city agencies, not surprisingly, were large and self-aggrandizing.

All four cities also collected extensive citizen suggestions for projects. Unlike earlier urban renewal project area committees and Model Cities boards, which limited participation by citizens to residents of target areas, CDBG broadened the membership and extended the scope of formal citizen involvement from the neighborhood to the city. Every city furthermore went beyond HUD's minimum citizen participation requirements for two public hearings. At one time or another during the first three years of the program, each city had a board of citizens charged with recommending projects to meet local needs. The result of all these features was a significantly expanded citizen participation process that generated a large number of proposed projects.

In fact, if any single fact characterized the agenda-setting process, it was that each city had far more demands for projects than there was money available. According to one New London official, "It was like a pot of gold had showed up." During the first year of the program, for example, New London officials faced $40 million in demands for $6.1 million in CDBG funds.

The character of these demands varied with the city's previous experience with similar programs. In the less active cities, the demands were mixed: city agencies requested money for their projects, and individual citizens made suggestions for neighborhood improvements. But in the more active cities, the demands were more numerous, more vocal, and more dominated by organizations: redevelopment agencies, city departments, neighborhood antipoverty agencies, and local public service groups. Compared with the less experienced cities, the more active cities also had more demands for public-service projects. Model Cities agencies expected to continue their projects, and new agencies sought a share of the largesse. The more experienced cities had also participated more actively in the federal antipoverty programs of the 1960s; in an era of declining federal support for these programs, local antipoverty agencies in these cities looked to CDBG as a way to secure a continuing source of income.

The nature of the demands, furthermore, tended to vary by neighborhood. Residents of higher income neighborhoods came to public meetings with requests for physical improvement of their neighborhoods, principally parks and public-works projects. Residents of lower-income neighborhoods, on the other hand, favored public-service projects, usually neighborhood-based projects such as day care services and improved health care. Some lower-income residents, particularly from several New Haven neighborhoods, also demanded projects to rehabilitate their houses. Demands for public services from lower-income neighborhoods, however, were far more numerous and vocal.

The demands of higher-income residents are not hard to understand. But why should lower-income families, often living in deteriorating neighborhoods and in housing of low quality, ask for public services instead of improvements in housing?

The answer is threefold. First, lower-income families rarely owned their own houses. A New Haven official commented:

> People in poor neighborhoods tend not to own their
> own homes, they tend to rent, so their concern with
> . . . upgrading these residences tends to be mini-
> mal—not that they wouldn't like to have better hous-
> ing, it's just that they have no direct control over
> providing it.

Second, public-service problems tended to be more immediate than long-range housing conditions. Another New Haven official said, "I think their social service problems are more immediate to them: What do I do with my kid who is on drugs?" Finally, and perhaps most importantly, public-service projects meant jobs in poor neighborhoods. The costs of these projects were largely salaries, and employees came mainly from the neighborhoods. Simply put by one New Haven official, "public-service projects are generally interpreted to mean jobs."

The mayors also often made proposals of their own. John Mandanici of Bridgeport proposed a new Waterfront Park to remove decaying industrial facilities from the city's waterfront and transform it into a park. New Haven's Frank Logue advocated a

Neighborhood Preservation Project to rehabilitate deteriorating
housing in several city neighborhoods.

The result was a complex set of demands from city agencies
for projects to foster their own growth and demands from citizens
for short-term, small-scale, neighborhood-based projects. But
most importantly, demands for projects far exceeded available funds.

Narrowing the Choices

The comprehensive planning approach that many CDBG advo-
cates envisioned never materialized. One New London official
explained: "From my experience, I haven't seen too much evidence
of [planning]. . . . It is like a big grab bag. We didn't really say
what we needed." In Bridgeport, one official said that as for planning,

> It ain't goin' on, and that's causing the system to deal
> with fragments of the program without being able to
> step back and see if the overall management system
> is geared to promote efficiency and to integrate CD
> with the other programs [in the city].

Norwich was "just responding to immediate needs," one planner conceded, and the lack of planning in New Haven, according to an administrator, "illustrates the severe weakness that we have in the
management process. . . . There is no assurance that [the CDBG
program] will be tied together in a unified way."

New Haven Mayor Frank Logue and his staff made the most
ambitious attempt to plan. After taking office in January 1976, they
began a thorough review, especially in public services, of former
Mayor Guida's proposals for second-year CDBG funding. Logue's
Human Resources Administrator Hugh Price proposed two functional
areas as top priority for CDBG public-service funds: youth services,
to attack the increasing problem of juvenile crime; and elderly
services, to meet the needs of a growing population of senior citizens. Price and his staff drafted a "Human Services Strategy" that
attempted to develop "a rational plan and a coordinated network of
services."[1] Furthermore, Price pledged to end the independence
of public-service agencies and to bring them under the control of
city hall.

Price's list of proposed projects contained three categories.
The first two—youth services and elderly services—included agencies
that met Price's strategy and that had agreed to work closely with
city hall. The third strategy was an amalgam of the previous year's

projects, which because of their support could not be cut, and of new proposals that had developed a large constituency. But a city official who had watched the development of both "plans" said he found Price's strategy little different from Guida's. Stripped of rhetoric, he said, it would be difficult to argue that either list represented a more "rational" or "comprehensive" set of projects to meet the city's needs. This is not to say that there are not other criteria on which one list might be superior; indeed, as we shall see in the next chapter, Logue demanded more results from his projects than did Guida. But given New Haven's needs, neither list of projects represented a demonstrably superior identification of priorities.

It would probably have been impossible for anyone, even with unlimited resources, to construct a comprehensive, "rational," plan for the optimal use of a city's CDBG funds. The needs were so great, the amount of funds available so small, and the objective criteria so vague as to make rational planning an unrealistic dream. For example, did New Haven, with substantial juvenile delinquency problems and deteriorating housing for low-income families need a crime prevention project more than housing rehabilitation? Did New London, with a declining central business district and obsolete fire stations that could not hold modern fire apparatus, need a downtown revitalization project more than a new fire station? It would be hard to imagine objective criteria that would give policy makers definitive answers to these questions.

Within the constraints that policy makers faced in the cities— a scarcity of skilled staff, scarce time, and competition with other demands and other programs in the city—a planned solution was impossible. As one public service planner in the New London-Norwich area explained, "There is no scientific, objective way" to set priorities and allocate funds. "There is a basic fallacy in trying to do it," he said.[2]

Each of the cities had a collection of old plans from earlier programs (including urban renewal, Model Cities, and state-funded community development programs). In the more experienced cities, the reservoir was larger because of the broader range of past activity. None of the plans had been completed, and city agencies consequently had shelves of ideas for CDBG projects. The concern of New London residents for the Bank Street area, for example, stretched back into the 1950s; the area had been under study for 25 years before the start of the Bank Street Project. Existing plans, one city official explained, brought certain preconceptions to the CDBG process about what areas deserved the most attention and what kind of projects should take place. But although the plans focused attention on particular neighborhoods and approaches, they did not determine the allocation of CDBG funds.

Instead, officials relied on what one local staff member called the "nifty-idea-I'm-for-that" approach to planning. It operated like this: "A housing rehabilitation project? That's a nifty idea! I'm for that!" The projects that received funding were those sufficiently attractive to build a broad base of political support.

But there were few interests that in themselves were sufficiently glamorous to attract a consensus. Even street tree planting to beautify a downtown area had detractors who either wanted the trees planted on their own street or wanted the funds spent on some other project altogether. Chief executives, citizens, and administrators played key roles in finally narrowing the choices.

Chief executive. In the cities with mayors (Bridgeport and New Haven), the mayor's role was potentially as large as he chose to make it. The mayors, however, chose to make that role relatively small because of the potential risks: with so many demands for projects, he risked making many enemies for every friend he made through a CDBG project grant. They limited themselves instead to setting broad goals and choosing pet projects. With much other pressing city business, the political volatility of the CDBG program, and the program's enormous complexity (with nearly 100 projects per year), one New Haven official said of the mayor, "He can't do more than establish general priorities." The mayor's concerns, therefore, lay more with favorite projects than with the program as a whole.

The city managers (in New London and Norwich) played a broader role in helping to structure the CDBG allocations. They put together a set of recommendations (even though the result was still far from a comprehensive program), but because they lacked the political standing of a mayor they had less influence on individual parts of the program. Their influence lay in a knowledge of the program, of individual projects, and of predictable reactions of the members of the council. As a Norwich official said of the city manager, "He knows what the city council wants and he goes in that direction."

Citizens. The citizen participation committees had substantial influence on the content of CDBG applications. A member of New London's Citizens Advisory Committee said that the city council "did listen to us" and rated the committee's influence "very good." A Bridgeport administrator called the Citizens Union "very well organized and very effective." "They keep us honest," the official said. "They have gotten sophisticated enough that they know what the law calls for." Public hearings in the other cities generated ideas that eventually found their way into the applications.

In subsequent years, however, citizens found that ongoing projects had first call on CDBG funds. Turnout at both the public hearings and the meetings of the citizen committees declined. In

preparing for the third-year application in New Haven, the workshops often had more representatives of the city government present
than citizens. In Bridgeport, rapid turnover in membership on the
Citizens Union crippled the organization; it became difficult to get
a quorum and to school the new members in the intricacies of the
program.

The city participation committees, furthermore, were guaranteed frustration. They had position without authority: local
officials had established the committees to meet the law's requirements for citizen participation and to formalize citizen input into
the process. There was never a promise that the citizens' recommendations would be followed, and although the citizens scored
major successes (such as the major parks improvement project in
Bridgeport) the citizens suffered under a lack of real authority over
allocations—authority that they both wanted and expected. One city
council member in Bridgeport explained, "They sometimes forget
that they are an advisory group. They want to become part of
management." Bridgeport Mayor John Mandanici concurred and
argued, "They're overstepping their bounds—they're only advisory."
A New London official expressed similar views, saying, "They
don't like it because the [city] council doesn't accept all their recommendations. They can't accept that they're just an advisory
group."

The cities with formal citizen committees had higher levels
of citizen frustration, for the more formal the citizen participation
process, the higher citizens' expectations were raised about their
potential influence on final decisions. Citizens and neighborhood
organizations soon realized, however, that there was a more effective channel through which to influence the allocations, a point
to which we will return later.

Administrators. As a result of the reorganization and of the
shift in control of the funds to local elected officials, administrators
associated with the former categorical programs lost much of their
independence. Nevertheless, the administrators who provided staff
assistance for the CDBG program—officials of the new community
development offices in Bridgeport, New London, and Norwich and
Redevelopment Agency officials in New Haven—had significant influence over the allocation of funds.[3] They understood the program's
changing regulations and had friends in HUD to explain the agency's
latest interpretations. They knew the details of each of the large
number of projects included in each application. They prepared the
application itself and the required supporting documents. In short,
they alone had command of the details of the program.

These administrators significantly influenced the content of
the application. They drew together the demand for projects from

citizens, other agencies, and politicians into a single document.
Their knowledge of the program's intricacies, especially the eligibility requirements for projects, put them in a powerful position to
choose some projects and eliminate others for technical reasons,
objective knowledge, and subjective judgment. This knowledge also
put them in an excellent position to suggest projects of their own and
marshal evidence to support them.

The administrators in the end actually drafted the application.
They drew together a list of recommended projects in consultation
with the executive to insure that his pet projects were included and
that none of the projects violated the executive's general priorities.
They also often exercised their own political judgments to assemble
a collection of projects about which a strong enough coalition would
form to move it through the city council. The draft application then
went to the council for review and final approval.

Appeals

The city council in all four cities had a far broader role in the
CDBG program than in the earlier categorical programs. Previously, the council routinely approved the plans submitted by the
categorical agencies. In the CDBG program, however, the council
played a far more active role. In the council-manager cities (New
London and Norwich), the members of the council were the ultimate
elected officials in charge of the program, and some of them pursued their own pet projects. But in all four cities, the council
served principally as a board of appeals, a court of last resort.

The council members routinely approved most of the items in
the draft applications submitted to them,[4] but as the last point of
review before the city sent the application to HUD, public hearings
held by the council often became a major battleground. Organizations that had earlier received funds fought to keep their allocation.
Other organizations that had lost the earlier rounds struggled to win
a share of the money. Constituents deluged council members with
requests, as one Bridgeport council member explained:

> Everybody would like a little bit. Your constituents
> call and ask you how a particular district can get a . . .
> community service center and we can't even get a basket-
> ball court.
>
> In all the districts, [the council members'] con-
> stituents are calling and asking them to bring back at
> least a small portion of the money. Most of them are
> resigned to the fact that they cannot get a large portion

of the money because of the nature of the program.
But they do like to see something in return for their
tax dollars.

Public interest in the CDBG program was far stronger than in
the local general fund budget. Citizens perceived the general fund
budget as constrained by long-standing demands for continuing
municipal services like education, fire protection, and police services. On the other hand, citizens perceived the CDBG entitlement
(incorrectly) as a no-strings grant that local officials could distribute entirely as they pleased. This perception attracted far greater
citizen attention to the CDBG budget than to the cities' regular budget. During the hearings for New Haven's third-year application,
for example, 200 people appeared to argue over the $4 million ear-
marked for public-service projects out of the $17.5 million entitle-
ment. That same evening, only two speakers appeared at a public
hearing to discuss the city's $94 million general fund budget.

Citizen interest grew into conflict as the more experienced
cities allocated the public-service portion of the entitlement. The
council not only faced large demands from many organizations but
a long tradition of strife between city hall and the neighborhoods.
Proponents of the projects brought busloads of supporters to the
council chambers to demonstrate their support. Other agencies
brought clients to testify to the value of the services. Council
members supported their constituents' demands, and the result,
according to one New Haven council member, was that the board
"dealt with individual [projects] like little baubles on a Christmas
tree."[5] A New London newspaper called the city council's public
hearings "New London's Theatre of the Absurd" and concluded:
"The result of all this is more of a grab-bag than a plan, a loose
collection of unrelated ways to spend money rather than a unified
approach to solving the city's most acute problems."[6]

The Role of Bargaining

In the end, it was bargaining—among elected officials, citizens, city bureaus, and neighborhood agencies—that was the most
prominent feature of local decision making. No one individual or
group cared very deeply about the local CDBG program as a whole,
but a large number of interests fought very hard for individual
projects. For elected officials, it was usually a highly visible
community improvement project for which they hoped to take credit.
For city bureaus, it was a project to maintain or expand their
mission. For citizens and neighborhood agencies, it was a project

to maintain or expand city services in their area. For all, it was only a portion of the CDBG entitlement—the money they hoped to win for themselves—that held importance.

It was a situation that encouraged logrolling by both function and area. City council members balanced the demands of the redevelopment agencies with public-service demands of the neighborhoods. They also balanced similar functional demands—say, for parks—by distributing park development money among the neighborhoods.

How successful each interest was depended on two things: how forcefully it stated its case as the administrators and citizen groups consolidated the agenda of proposed projects into a draft application; and how strongly it defended itself before the city council as other groups struggled for a share of the funds. The strategies varied widely. Mayors explained how their pet projects would attack key city problems. Redevelopment agencies cited long-standing commitments to completing their projects. Neighborhood organizations marshaled clients to demonstrate public support for their services.

There was no central authority—mayor, city council, or citizen advisory group—that attempted to meld the individual projects into a comprehensive strategy. Instead, each interest group traded its support for other projects for a share of the money.

THE OUTCOME OF LOCAL DECISIONS

Over the first three years of the program, the cities spent most of their money for urban renewal, housing rehabilitation, neighborhood parks and facilities, and social services projects (see Table 5.1). The local bargaining process, furthermore, produced scattered, short-term, neighborhood-based projects. Local officials also showed an occasional inclination to use CDBG funds for tax relief.

Scattering

Compared with the geographically concentrated projects of the urban renewal and Model Cities programs, the CDBG program significantly increased the number of city neighborhoods receiving funds. One Bridgeport official explained, "everybody wants a piece of the pie, so you can't concentrate in a single area." Decision making in the CDBG program, according to New Haven Mayor Frank Logue, was "programming by area." In Bridgeport, for example,

TABLE 5.1

Allocation of Money by Function and City
(in percentages)

Function	Bridgeport	New Haven	New London	Norwich
Downtown renewal	2	2	24	0
Municipal services and equipment	0	0	12	2
Urban renewal	35	32	10	53
Housing rehabilitation	15	15	14	12
Neighborhood parks and facilities	16	4	6	2
Neighborhood public works	1	6	3	20
Social services	15	17	20	3
Planning and administration	12	17	9	3
Other	4	7	1	5
Total	100	100	99*	100
Amount (in millions of dollars)	$12.0	$54.5	$19.4	$4.4

*Total does not add due to rounding.
Source: Derived from proposed activities in local applications.

a park improvement project advocated by the city's citizen advisory committee gave a new park to every member's district. In New Haven, Mayor Bart Guida distributed money to each of the city's neighborhood corporations, whose support he sought to strengthen, shortly before his party's mayoral primary (which he lost to Frank Logue). Other projects, one Bridgeport official explained, were "appeasements—done to appease a certain group" in return for their support. The result, according to one New Haven city official, was a "crazy" collection of projects "sprinkled" around the city. In each city, at least two-thirds of the census tracts had

projects: 68 percent in Bridgeport; 69 percent in New Haven; 93
percent in New London; and 77 percent in Norwich.*

Short-Term Projects

With the CDBG program came the end of ten-year urban renewal projects. CDBG's neighborhood-based projects were short-
term, small-scale projects such as rehabilitation of individual
houses within a neighborhood or public-service projects funded for
a single year.
Part of the reason was the unstable, annual nature of the program. Cities had to submit a new application for funds each year,
and HUD changed its eligibility requirements from year to year.
As a result, the cities could not be sure for which projects they
would have money. Furthermore, since Congress originally had
authorized the program for only three years, none of the cities
knew with certainty how much money it would have in the future.
The result, according to a New Haven planner, is that officials
said to themselves, "I better pick things which are visible, things
which are certain to occur."
Part of the reason was also the biennial elections that constantly faced elected officials. One New London official explained:

> The program subjects itself to yearly citizen partici-
> pation and political pressure. The governing body
> is political and it is influenced by its constituency. . . .
> [Constituents want] immediate things . . . visible
> things. The politicians want a program before the next
> election.

New Haven's mayor, an aide explained, "takes the rap for what
goes wrong and is lauded for what goes right." The result was
strong pressure for quick results.

---

*Each project's location was identified by census tract. The
average annual entitlement that could thus be identified in each city
was: Bridgeport, 84 percent; New Haven, 37 percent (because of
a large number of citywide social service and housing rehabilitation
projects); New London, 77 percent; and Norwich, 93 percent. Planning, administration, and "other" costs account for most of the
remaining money.

Neighborhood-Based Projects

The focus of CDBG projects was the neighborhood. After accounting for planning and administrative costs and for the required completion of urban renewal projects, the cities spent nearly all of their remaining money on neighborhood-based services: housing rehabilitation, parks and facilities, public works, and social services. For the physical development projects, the money produced visible signs of the program's activity. For the social service projects, the money usually produced jobs for neighborhood residents. The key element uniting all these projects was an identifiable neighborhood stake in the CDBG program.

In the functional areas over which city officials had the most leeway in meeting neighborhood demands—housing rehabilitation, neighborhood parks and facilities, neighborhood public works, and social services—the cities' planned use of the money reflected citizen demands for neighborhood projects. (Money in the other functional categories either did not directly affect the neighborhoods or, in the case of urban renewal, represented the required completion of projects begun under the categorical programs.) Of the money allocated to parks and public works, the cities decided to spend most of the money in upper-income areas. On the other hand, most of the money for housing rehabilitation and especially for social services went to lower-income neighborhoods.

Table 5.2 shows the allocation of CDBG money by the four functional areas and by the income of the neighborhood in which the projects are located. In the neighborhood parks and facilities projects, the cities earmarked 58 percent of the money for upper-income neighborhoods; of neighborhood public-works funds, upper-income neighborhoods received 70 percent of the total. (Upper-income neighborhoods are those composed predominantly of census tracts with median incomes of more than 80 percent of the city median income.) On the other hand, 78 percent of housing rehabilitation money and an even larger 84 percent of social services funds went to lower-income neighborhoods (those composed predominantly of census tracts with median incomes of less than 80 percent of the city median income).

It should not be assumed that these figures represent the allocation of program benefits. Rather, they indicate the location of projects; some projects (like social services) located in upper-income neighborhoods may nevertheless benefit lower-income people living in poverty pockets and some projects located in lower-income neighborhoods (like a golf course) may predominantly benefit upper-income residents. But the figures do demonstrate the fragmented character of the program and the ability of city officials to

TABLE 5.2

Location of Projects by Function and Income of Neighborhood
(dollar amounts in thousands)

Income of Neighborhood*	Function			
	Rehabilitation	Neighborhood Parks and Facilities	Neighborhood Public Works	Social Services
Bridgeport	$1,762	$1,906	$75	$1,793
Lower income	80%	8%	0%	96%
Upper income	20%	92%	100%	4%
New Haven	$8,161	$2,087	$3,056	$9,408
Lower income	99%	53%	38%	81%
Upper income	1%	47%	62%	19%
New London	$2,620	$1,243	$664	$3,922
Lower income	25%	71%	36%	87%
Upper income	75%	29%	64%	13%
Norwich	$530	$75	$868	$147
Lower income	9%	67%	0%	0%
Upper income	91%	33%	100%	100%
All cities	$13,073	$5,311	$4,663	$15,270
Lower income	78%	42%	30%	84%
Upper income	22%	58%	70%	16%

*Lower-income neighborhoods are those composed predominantly of census tracts with median incomes of less than 80 percent of the city median income. Upper-income neighborhoods are composed predominantly of census tracts with median incomes of more than 80 percent of the city median income. Median income is taken from the 1970 Census.

Source: Derived from proposed activities in local applications.

link particular projects with identifiable constituencies—and to re-spond to citizen demands. The large share of park and public works projects for upper-income neighborhoods is particularly significant in light of HUD's continued efforts to force the cities to concentrate their CDBG funds in lower-income areas. The upper-income areas traded in the currency of physical improvements: lower-income neighborhoods took most of the money for housing rehabili-tation and social services.

Tax Relief

With the CDBG program responsible to a broader constituency than the categorical programs, one of the most immediate ways to appeal to a large group of citizens was by using the money to keep down the local tax rate. Program regulations forbade the use of funds to reduce the tax rate but a New London city council member saw the program this way:

> This money should not be wasted on foolish programs.
> It should be used for the benefit of all citizens of New
> London who are interested in a further reduction of
> the tax rate and programs that will benefit the entire
> city of New London and not just a few areas.[7]

Cities developed imaginative ways to use CDBG funds to keep the tax rate down. New London used CDBG money to purchase a building from itself and also allocated funds for the planned fire station. In Norwich, CDBG money "supplied the city's capital im-provement budget." The councilmen really see it as a way to keep the tax rate down," one city official explained.[8]

THE CONSEQUENCES FOR LOCAL POLITICS

New Conflicts for Elected Officials

The CDBG brought a new type of political conflict to the cities. The money was highly visible and many local residents—both elected officials and citizens—looked on the program as "new," "no strings" money (even though Congress had enacted the program to replace the categorical programs and had insisted on some restraints on local discretion). In addition, the program's ambitious and exten-sive citizen participation brought huge demands for new projects. The CDBG allocation process, furthermore, lay outside the cities' regular budgetary process and was not constrained by ongoing local programs.

These circumstances posed enormous political problems for the local elected officials, particularly the mayors. They had broad discretion on how to spend the money. But for every friend they made with a dollar spent they made many more enemies among groups whose requests went unanswered. For every project that received funds, there were often four or five others—with their own supporters—that did not. By putting local elected officials at the focus of competing demands yet giving them the resources to meet only some of them, the program placed local elected officials in an extraordinarily vulnerable position.

Even before the passage of the program, Floyd Hyde, former mayor of Fresno, California, and former Assistant HUD Secretary for Community Development, warned that mayors were already uncomfortable in the increased discretion promised them. His former mayoral colleagues, he said, vocally supported greater discretion. But they also took him aside and confided: "For God['s] sake, don't let it happen that way. We need some guidance, where we can lean on the Feds and say they made us do it in this area for that purpose."[9] In granting greater discretion to local governments, the program ironically took from local officials a source of comfort: the ability to use the dictates of federal programs and officials as a screen behind which to make politically unpopular decisions. CDBG put local elected officials squarely on the spot for making program policy.

In all four cities, elected officials tried to centralize the process for making decisions. Mayors campaigned strongly for their pet projects. Council members advanced their own favorite projects and tried where possible to win a share of the program's benefits for their own constituency. But elected officials shrunk from trying to impose a broad strategy on the local CDBG program. Instead, they exhibited symptoms of what Anthony Downs called the "Shrinking Violet Syndrome"[10] and Jeffrey L. Pressman labeled "conflict avoidance."[11] A consultant to several cities in the program explained, "most mayors don't like to make these decisions about where to spend this money." A New Haven official added, "Political types don't like to make decisions. As soon as you start making decisions, you automatically start alienating people." When greater discretion became a reality, elected officials in the four cities performed as did members of Oakland's city council, as described by Pressmen: they pursued "a consistent policy of actively giving up jurisdiction in areas which [they considered] troublesome."[12] The officials pressed for a small set of pet projects but they mostly surrendered their authority over the remainder of the entitlement.

A Broader Role for Citizens and Interest Groups

No previous federal program had given such a broad group of citizens such extensive chances for influencing the distribution of federal money. To be sure, some of the War on Poverty programs established bastions of considerable power in the neighborhoods, but participation was generally limited to residents of "target" neighborhoods. [13] Citizen-participation committees in the urban renewal and Model Cities programs were aimed at those likely to be affected by the programs. The CDBG program, by contrast, opened participation to the entire community. Since the program's regulations did not categorically exclude any neighborhood from receiving funds, few neighborhoods did not have representatives requesting funds.

CDBG citizen participation, furthermore, proved influential at least as measured by the ability of some citizens to have their proposals funded. Sometimes the influence rested on the force of numbers with busloads of supporters arguing for a project. Sometimes the influence rested on citizens winning the ear of their council member who then succeeded in bringing back a piece of the pie. And sometimes the influence rested on voters living in a neighborhood that a mayor wanted to win. But in the end, citizens' voices were heard, and the allocation decisions at least to some degree reflected their demands.

To speak properly about citizen participation we must speak about citizen groups. Although individual citizens did often appear to ask for new street lights or removal of a crumbling building, groups of citizens—often noisy and rambunctious—dominated citizen-participation meetings and city council hearings. They also were most influential in the allocation decisions.

Local claimant organizations dominated the CDBG budget process. Some were city bureaus, like the redevelopment agencies and public-works departments. Others were neighborhood-level organizations left over from the War on Poverty for whom the projects meant jobs and continued political power, power that ironically earlier federal grant programs had given them. Still others were private agencies like the YMCA or Big Brothers-Big Sisters. But all were struggling to maintain what Graham T. Allison called "organizational health"—maintaining (and if possible, increasing) the number of their employees, the scope of their services, and the size of their budgets. [14]

Considerable Power for Local Administrators

It was a difficult time for the organizations that had previously dominated community development agencies. The CDBG program put Model Cities agencies out of business and redevelopment agencies, which had grown accustomed to long-term projects and easy application amendments, discovered that they now had to fight for a meager portion from a smaller pot. The program mandated the conclusion of previously approved urban renewal projects but even winning this money sometimes meant a battle.

Furthermore, one of the program's goals clearly was to wrest program control from these semiautonomous agencies and place responsibility in the hands of elected officials. We reviewed the arguments for this change in Chapter 1: that the agencies had become independent fiefdoms with closer ties to their functional allies in Washington than to the officials of their cities. Redevelopment agencies could no longer run their projects within an arena separate from other local struggles. In the two cities with less categorical program experience and hence less powerful redevelopment agencies, local elected officials totally shut out the agencies from the planning and administration of the CDBG program. The lack of funds for any new projects and the establishment of new community development agencies meant exile and perhaps eventual death for the redevelopment agencies.

In the two cities with larger and more experienced redevelopment agencies, however, the agencies may have lost some independence, but they scarcely lost power. New London's redevelopment agency took on execution of the Bank Street plans. In New Haven, the redevelopment agency directed most of the large physical development projects (including the Taft Hotel conversion and Neighborhood Preservation). New Haven's redevelopment agency also took on the general administrative responsibilities for the program.

Whichever city agency took on these administrative chores also gained substantial power in the program. (In all cities but New Haven, this agency was a new community development bureau.) The program's regulations were vague and constantly shifting; officials who could interpret the current state of the program were invaluable. Eligibility standards for projects were particularly troublesome and one local administrator would sit behind a desk deciding, in a matter-of-fact way, whether he could "make this project eligible." Project eligibility was often less a fact than a bargained outcome. Administrators with the knowledge of the projects and good contacts with federal officials played far more than a neutral role in preparing the grant application.

This knowledge was particularly valuable to elected officials who found themselves at the center of overwhelming demands. Elected officials could defend a decision not to fund a project if one of the administrators declared a project ineligible. For elected officials trying to avoid conflict, local bureaucrats could therefore be important allies. And since the complexity and ambiguity of the program's regulations gave the administrators ample room to exercise their own discretion, the program that set out to concentrate power in the hands of elected officials also gave considerable power to program administrators.

LOCAL ALLOCATION OF FEDERAL MONEY

Two Views of Local Performance

Two views are possible on the process by which the cities allocated their federal money.

On one hand, it can be argued that the cities performed well. Each city made substantial commitments to major projects addressing what citizens and local officials perceived as its worst problems: New Haven had a major housing rehabilitation project; Bridgeport, a waterfront development project; New London and Norwich, downtown revitalization projects. Most of the remaining money met legitimate community development needs. Some of the money funded some functions that were ineligible under earlier federal assistance programs. Some of the money went for projects in neighborhoods outside the narrow geographic boundaries of the categorical programs. Some of the money went for short-term municipal service needs (like street repair) that the cities could not have met with local tax revenues. The cities' needs were so great, in fact, that it was almost (but only almost) impossible to spend the money badly.

Local decisions, furthermore, were responsive to the needs citizens described. No federal program in recent history has given individual citizens greater potential to influence the distribution of such large sums of money. And as we have seen, the influence of citizens, both individually and organized in groups, on the allocation of funds was substantial. Despite the protests by citizen committee members that decision makers were ignoring them and despite the shrillness that often accompanied their demands, CDBG allocations showed a close correspondence with the demands made on the money. There were important qualifications to the openness of the process: the organizational resources of some city agencies gave them an advantage in the competition for funds; and city officials were often unsure exactly whom the so-called neighborhood representatives actually represented. But local CDBG allocations, it could be argued, were on the whole both reasonable and responsive.

On the other hand, four criticisms can be made about their decisions.

First, some of the money went to "buy off" some citizens and neighborhoods with tennis courts, parks, and sidewalks. These projects were the political price paid for other projects.

Second, the cities gave little recognition to problems above the neighborhood level. In funding neighborhood-based projects, the cities made little attempt to grapple with problems that spanned the neighborhoods. And the cities made no attempt to use their CDBG entitlements to deal with problems they shared with neighboring cities.

Third, even within the neighborhoods the cities made no attempt to coordinate CDBG projects. The unspoken demand hidden in each fund request was for autonomy, and successful applicants expected to be able to follow their own agendas—not to have other agencies' agendas forced on them. Local officials made few attempts to gain control over individual projects or to establish potential links between projects. The local CDBG application was no more than a fragmented collection of individual projects.

Fourth, the cities made few attempts to identify their most important needs or to compare the relative advantages of competing projects. Even limited planning to identify key features of projects—often including their likely cost—did not occur. And if it was hard to spend money badly, it was important to spend it well. The cities never conducted the planning needed to separate the good from the better project proposals.

These criticisms are not specific to these four cities. As we saw in Chapter 2, a host of monitoring reports found similar problems in the CDBG program across the country. Other block grant programs, especially the Comprehensive Employment and Training Act, have also been attacked for inadequate planning and for failure to spend the money on national goals.[15]

How can we reconcile these conflicting interpretations of local performance? Can the cities be trusted with great discretion over large sums of money? Or does prudent management demand close federal supervision of local governments? Our examination of these four cities leads to no definitive answer.

Perhaps the better question is: with what can the cities be trusted? To that question we have a much clearer answer. The cities spent their money on projects that were important at least to those elected officials making the decisions. Elected officials, furthermore, matched the projects to the demands of their citizens. They were also able to use the money flexibly to tackle short-term problems that might otherwise have gone unsolved. But these results did not come without costs. Local planning was nearly nonexistent. Selection of projects instead depended on the "nifty-idea-I'm-for-that" approach that in turn relied on developing projects with immediate appeals for identifiable constituencies. The local "plan" consequently was no more than a collection of individual projects that took little account of national program objectives.

The Distributive Politics of Community Development

Both the process and the outcome of community development decisions were different in the CDBG program than in the previous categorical programs. The categorical programs, particularly urban renewal and Model Cities, were essentially redistributive programs designed to concentrate federal aid according to greatest need. The process of making decisions was centralized (in federal rather than local hands) and bureaucratized (in administrative rather than in elected officials' hands). The decision process, furthermore, concentrated federal money narrowly within carefully defined neighborhoods. Whether in fact the categoricals concentrated the money on the most important needs is a debatable point.[16] The categoricals did, however, centralize, bureaucratize, and concentrate federal money at the local level, especially in comparison with the CDBG program.

The CDBG program, by contrast, turned out in practice to be essentially a distributive program that spread federal money broadly around city neighborhoods. The process of making decisions was decentralized (with large responsibility in local hands) and open to a wide range of influences. The process, furthermore, was reactive: rather than develop a consistent strategy for the money, local elected officials responded to the demands placed on them.[17] The result was the pattern of scattered, short-term, neighborhood-based projects we saw earlier.[18]

The CDBG program thus was not simply another strategy for achieving the same goals as the previous categorical programs. It was a program with a much different process and a distinctive set of outcomes. It was a program that equipped the cities to deal flexibly with the widely varying community development problems they faced. But other problems, particularly those that would demand longer commitments (like long-term economic development), redistribution of income to the poor, or concentration of funds in a narrow functional area (like housing), were beyond local capacity. The time horizon of local officials was too short and the demand for widespread distribution of benefits was too great to allow local governments to launch a concerted attack on these problems.

In the next chapter, we will examine what happened after the cities set their budgets: how they executed the projects they chose.

NOTES

1. New Haven Human Resources Administration, "Human Services Strategy for Second Year Community Development Entitlement" (March 1976), p. 2.

2. For a description of the urban decision-making environment and the impossibility of planning, see Douglas Yates, The Ungovernable City: The Politics of Urban Problems and Policy Making (Cambridge, Mass.: MIT Press, 1977); and Willis D. Hawley and David Rogers, eds., Improving the Quality of Urban Management (Beverly Hills: Sage Publications, 1974).

3. For a similar argument, see Victor Bach's testimony, U.S. Congress, House, Committee on Banking, Finance and Urban Affairs, Housing and Community Development Act of 1977, Hearings before the Subcommittee on Housing and Community Development of the Committee on Banking, Housing and Currency, 95th Cong., 1st sess., 1977, p. 642; and Richard P. Nathan et al., Block Grants for Community Development (Washington, D.C.: U.S. Department of Housing and Community Development, January 1977), p. 397.

4. The Brookings study on the program found a similar result in their sample of cities. See Nathan et al., Block Grants for Community Development, pp. 373-84.

5. New Haven Advocate, April 20, 1977.

6. New London Day, January 31, 1976.

7. New London Day, September 23, 1974.

8. These patterns in process and outcome replicate similar findings produced by other studies of the CDBG program. See, for example, the testimony of Victor Bach before the Subcommittee on Banking, Finance and Urban Affairs, Housing and Community Development Act of 1977, especially pp. 638-39; and Nathan et al., Block Grants for Community Development.

Students of other block grant programs have likewise found a "growing politicization of the planning process." See U.S. Advisory Commission on Intergovernmental Relations, The Comprehensive Employment and Training Act: Early Readings from a Hybrid Block Grant (Washington, D.C.: U.S. Government Printing Office, June 1977), p. 43. For views on other block grant programs, see these ACIR studies: The Partnership for Health Act: Lessons from a Pioneering Block Grant (Washington, D.C.: U.S. Government Printing Office, January 1977), especially pp. 122-23; and Safe Streets Reconsidered: The Block Grant Experience 1968-1975 (Washington, D.C.: U.S. Government Printing Office, January 1977), especially p. 80.

A task force appointed by the Attorney General also contended that intended planning under the law enforcement block grant, "was not taking place." See the Department of Justice Study Group, Report to the Attorney General: Restructuring the Justice Department's Program of Assistance to State and Local Governments for Crime Control and Criminal Justice System Improvement (Washington, D.C.: June 23, 1977), pp. 7-9.

9. Testimony, U.S. Congress, Senate, Committee on Banking, Housing and Urban Affairs, Community Development Block Grant Program, Hearings before the Committee on Banking, Housing and Urban Affairs, 94th Cong., 2d sess., 1976, p. 574.

10. Anthony Downs, Inside Bureaucracy (Boston: Little, Brown, 1967), p. 217.

11. Jeffrey L. Pressman, Federal Programs and City Politics: The Dynamics of the Aid Process in Oakland (Berkeley: University of California Press, 1975), p. 40. See also Matthew Holden, Jr., "'Imperialism' in Bureaucracy," American Political Science Review 60 (December 1966): 943-51.

12. Pressman, Federal Programs and City Politics, p. 40.

13. For one view of these programs, see Daniel P. Moynihan, Maximum Feasible Misunderstanding: Community Action in the War on Poverty (New York: Free Press, 1970.

14. Graham T. Allison, The Essence of Decision: Explaining the Cuban Missile Crisis (Boston: Little, Brown, 1971), p. 82.

15. For a summary view of all of the block grant programs, see the U.S. Advisory Commission on Intergovernmental Relations, Block Grants: A Comparative Analysis (Washington, D.C.: U.S. Government Printing Office, 1977).

16. For a sample of the debate on urban renewal, see James Q. Wilson, ed., Urban Renewal: The Record and the Controversy (Cambridge, Mass.: MIT Press, 1966).

17. For a thorough exploration of reactive politics in cities, see Douglas Yates, The Ungovernable City: The Politics of Urban Problems and Policy Making (Cambridge, Mass.: MIT Press, 1977).

18. These distinctions between distributive and redistributive politics draw heavily on Theodore J. Lowi, "American Business, Public Policy, Case-Studies, and Political Theory," World Politics 16 (July 1964): 677-715.

6
EXECUTING THE PROJECTS

THE TRIALS OF PROJECT EXECUTION

Broad Range of Results

The cities' problems scarcely ended when the raucous city council meetings ended. Budgeting the money and executing the plans were two far different things. The budgeting process was concerned almost entirely with distributional questions: who is getting how much money for which projects? Questions about how the projects would be executed rarely even entered the arena. In fact, as we shall discover shortly, the amount of money allocated to a project sometimes was not even related to how much the project would cost. Executing the projects became a task of negotiating pitfalls along a rocky road, with some of the obstacles created by the budgeting process itself.

The four cities had an extraordinarily broad range of results. Among the eight project case studies in Chapters 3 and 4 were glowing successes and outright failures. On one hand, New London's newspaper praised the Bank Street project for bringing back the city's halcyon days. On the other hand, Norwich never even broke ground for the Rose Tower project. In between the extremes were projects that covered the spectrum.

Even within a single city the outcomes varied. While New London's Bank Street project brought people back downtown, for example, the city council abandoned plans for a new fire station because of growing citizen opposition.

What accounts for such a wide range of outcomes? Why did some cities more effectively execute their projects than other cities?

And within the cities, why did officials have far more success with some projects than others? The answers rest on two features of local performance.

First, the program imposed new general management responsibilities on the cities. Local governments took on many administrative tasks formerly performed in whole or in part by HUD. For the first time, the cities were solely responsible for reviewing the efficacy of their own plans. They had to develop a central office for managing the program's details. And for the first time, the cities had to devise procedures for assuring and documenting their compliance with general federal standards: environmental reviews, equal employment opportunity, wage standards, and many others. The wide range of outcomes was due in part to the greater skill some cities showed in solving the program's general management problems.

Second, each project within the cities posed special management problems. Some projects, like public works, were comparatively easy to execute because they fit in with established procedures in existing city agencies. Some projects, however, were far more complicated, like New Haven's plan to renovate the Hotel Taft. Furthermore, some of the cities proved more adept than others in handling complicated projects. The wide range of outcomes was thus also due to project-based features: the complexity of each project and the city's ability to manage that complexity.

The Problem of Delay

How well the cities handled these two problems determined how well they overcame the foremost pathology of the execution process: delay—sometimes short, often long, and occasionally fatal.[1] A convoluted array of unforeseen problems conspired to slow or even to halt some projects. City officials managed to conquer the problems in other projects. But for each project, the combination of general CDBG management burdens and specific project details made project execution hardly a sure thing and sometimes even made spending CDBG funds difficult.*

In the following pages, we will examine the cities' execution of their CDBG projects according to the most simple of tests: their ability to fulfill project plans. There are, of course, far more

---

*Since the public-service project budgets consisted largely of salaries, it was rarely hard to spend the money.

stringent standards by which to judge local implementation. We will discover, however, that even according to this simple test, the cities demonstrated a wide range of administrative capacity.

GENERAL MANAGEMENT PROBLEMS

Before work could begin on individual projects, each city had to cross three hurdles. First, since the cities only rarely had more than a general description of projects before they sent their applications to HUD for approval, each city had to develop specific plans for each project. Furthermore, each city had to develop a management system—a set of procedures by which the city could accomplish routine tasks. HUD also had its own set of general requirements that the cities had to fulfill before the department would release funds for each project.

Developing Details

The amount of money a project received rarely reflected more than a project's relative priority. The focus of the CDBG budget process was on who got the money rather than what the money would buy, on inputs rather than outputs.[2] Project proposals that city officials collected usually consisted only of a one- or two-sentence description of the project. Sometimes decision makers had just a project title. As a result, only scanty details of individual projects were available to guide implementation. City officials often were not even sure that the money budgeted for a project would cover its cost. "You write something on a plan to HUD," one local official explained, "but that doesn't mean it's a project. A lot of the planning hasn't been done."

One New Haven official, for example, described the steps leading to the implementation of the Neighborhood Preservation Project. The city administration, he said, decided on the $3 million figure like this: "Let's put a lot of money into that project. How about $3 million? That sounds good." In Norwich, the city earmarked $400,000 for the Falls Project, not because that was how much their planned activities would cost (for they did not know specifically what they wanted to do with the money) but because the amount represented their view of the project's priority.

This process created problems in executing the projects. Local officials could not begin work on the projects until they decided precisely what the project was to accomplish: what houses would be rehabilitated, where a fire station would be built, or how a street would be redirected. It was not until after HUD approved local applications that the cities began developing details of the projects.

This problem, of course, is specific neither to the CDBG program nor to the cities. Hugh Heclo noted in his study of executive politics in Washington that "policies are often bundles of mutual understandings rather than clearly spelled-out directives."[3] The bargaining process that characterized CDBG budgeting often produced only mutual understandings of the projects' relative priority. It yielded little to guide administrative officials who would have to carry out the projects.

The vagueness of project plans gave administrators wide discretion in developing the details. The discretion was not unchecked for, as we saw, citizens sometimes argued extensively over the location of a fire station or the signs over downtown stores. The result as administrators struggled to work out these project details was delay.

Management Systems

Each city also faced the task of developing a general system to manage its CDBG entitlement. The grants were sometimes enormous compared to local budgets: in New London, the grant was one-half the size of the city's general fund budget; in New Haven, one-fifth; in Norwich, one-twelfth; and in Bridgeport, one-twentieth. Strictly in terms of the amount of money, the CDBG program was big business in the cities. And the big business brought new problems because for the first time the program concentrated local management for federal community development programs under one roof—city hall.

The first question was basic: who would control the money? Local elected officials decided quickly that control would remain in their hands. But elected officials realized that they could not run the entire program themselves; they would have to rely on some combination of new and existing agencies, both municipal and community-based, to implement the varied mixture of CDBG projects.

One alternative was to delegate the administrative chores to the redevelopment agencies, which had years of experience in dealing with HUD and with large sums of federal money. Local officials, however, were not eager to surrender control to the redevelopment agencies of any but redevelopment projects. In the end, the cities left central administrative responsibilities to the same agencies that prepared the applications: in Bridgeport, New London, and Norwich, it was the new community development office; in New Haven, ironically, it was the redevelopment agency. These agencies acted as the prime agents for management control, from checking on project progress to supervising accounting and record-keeping.

The cities found that they could rely on existing municipal operations for many other chores. They incorporated existing personnel, purchasing, and accounting procedures into the CDBG program. Many city agencies, furthermore, had years of experience in hardware projects: paving streets, building parks, or pouring sidewalks. The redevelopment agencies, of course, had their own mechanisms for renewal projects.

In public services, however, the bewildering number and variety of projects went far past the existing administrative structure of the city governments. None of the cities wanted to get involved in directly administering all of the social-service projects. Local officials knew they could not count on a long-range commitment from the federal government to sustain the projects, and they did not want to build up a large new city agency to administer the projects. They not only feared that the city itself might have to pick up the operating costs of such an agency but that the city might also be pressured into continuing the social service projects indefinitely from municipal revenues.*

Furthermore, many of the neighborhood organizations that received funds fully expected independence from city hall in their operations. Some of the organizations had sprung from the "neighborhood control" era of the 1960s. Others had produced a show of political force before the city council and expected to have a free hand. Still others believed that they knew their neighborhood's needs far better than anyone in city hall. Agencies with a citywide base had their own ideas about how services should be delivered.

City officials nevertheless had no intention of allowing CDBG-funded neighborhood organizations complete autonomy. Not only were the cities legally responsible to HUD for the management of the program, but they also wanted to make sure that the city got something in return for the money. Several neighborhood groups, furthermore, had long histories of mismanagement, particularly in fiscal affairs. Neighborhood organizations in New Haven had faced constant problems from audits on other federal and state projects; the problems eventually led to one organization's exclusion from further funding. In New London, the local newspaper uncovered

---

*Norwich is excluded from this analysis of public-service management because it did not have a significant number of public-service projects.

problems ranging from no-interest loans for employees to excessive paid vacations. One New London city official, in fact, concluded, "Some of the agencies just don't have the capabilities or the
knowledge to administer funds." A Bridgeport official concurred:
"We find sometimes an inability of the operating agencies to administer the projects."

The cities thus faced a complicated problem: allowing these
agencies the operating flexibility that they demanded while also controlling their performance, since it was the city itself that was ulti-
mately responsible to HUD for the money. To deal with the problem
the cities resorted to detailed contracts. City officials defined the
services that the agency would perform and stipulated the conditions
under which the agency would be paid.

The contracting strategy produced other problems in turn.
First, the city officials charged with developing the contracts had
little experience with the contract as a management tool. Consequently, it took them weeks, in some cases months, to puzzle out
an approach, to decide how the contract should be negotiated, and
to produce a CDBG contract form.

Second, the key element of the contract, the "scope of services," defied careful definition. Unlike the contract for a road or
a building, in which the city could make clear engineering specifications, the "scope" for a public-service project was necessarily
more nebulous. Not only was there no clear technical language for
communicating the measurement standards for public-service goals
(compared with, say, the gauge of wire for an electrical installa-
tion), but there was also often only a vague sense of what public-
service projects should accomplish. The administering agencies
eventually produced contracts to meet these problems. But the contracts sometimes went little past a charge to serve the poor and, as
one Bridgeport official complained, "it takes a hell of a long time to
get a contract [signed]."

City officials had even more difficulty in trying to find out
what all of the operating agencies were doing with the money. The
cities relied on two sources. They required first that their contractors file regular reports on the progress of CDBG projects.
Physical development contractors could report that they had completed 65 percent of a project or that they were awaiting delivery of
steel. Public-service contractors, on the other hand, could report
that they had "served" 75 individuals in the previous month. These
public-service reports would tell city officials that the projects were
operating, however, without really telling them how effectively.
City officials also occasionally wondered whether the numbers were
manufactured for their benefit. Many of the public-service contractors, furthermore, resisted the city's demand for reports

claiming, "We're so busy providing services we don't have time to push that paper."

The cities therefore also developed a procedure for paying monitoring visits to the site of the projects. City officials would come to the project, examine the records, survey the activities, and write a report about how well they believed the project met its goals (as defined in the contract). The monitoring visits occasionally produced surprising results—the discovery by city officials that a swimming instructor was giving no swimming lessons or that a large youth recreation project existed only on paper.

The contractors predictably resented city officials snooping into their projects. One city official called the relationship with contractors "rocky" and another said that "it's caused some tensions" because the contractors resented "anyone looking over their shoulders." In time, however, "people got used to the system [and] the quality of the services . . . improved," he said.

More serious than the resistance to "snooping," however, was the lack of manpower to monitor the projects adequately. In New Haven, for example, there were 63 public-service projects funded during the third year; only two staff members had even partial responsibility for monitoring. Although the number of projects and monitoring manpower varied by town, the problem was universal. City officials had time for only a brief visit to each project and then not more than once or twice during each year. Consequently, city officials had only minimal knowledge of what was happening with CDBG public-service funds.

The most taxing of the requirements was the review by local governments of the environmental impact of each project. The National Environmental Policy Act of 1969 required the federal government to measure the environmental impact of all federal projects. In the CDBG program, however, the federal government for the first time delegated to subnational governments the environmental review responsibility.

Environmental review built an automatic delay of at least 35 days into every project. Once a city decided on the details of a project (itself often the cause of delays), it had to decide whether the project was likely to have a significant impact on the environment and publish the findings. If the city decided that a project had no significant environmental impact, it could publish a second notice 15 days later advising the public that it was about to request HUD to release the funds. Five days later the city could ask HUD to release funds for the project; 15 days after receiving the city's request—a minimum of 35 days after the beginning of the process—HUD could release the funds. If the city found that the project would have a significant effect (a relatively rare event that occurred for only 75 projects nationwide in the first two years of the program), the city had to prepare a full environmental impact statement (itself a major undertaking) and the minimum review period extended to 110 days.

The built-in delays at each step gave interested citizens and agencies a chance to file written complaints with both HUD and the city before work began on a project that might harm the environment. City officials, however, pointed out that the process had a "hair-trigger"—an objection from one citizen could halt a project. Other critics of the process complained that the very openness of the review reduced the likelihood that an agency would look very carefully at the environmental issues for fear of exposing the agency to legal harassment. [4]

Furthermore, the act required local governments to review the environmental impact of projects that obviously had no effect on the environment. Bridgeport, for example, delayed a dental screening project for youngsters to assess its impact on the environment. The General Accounting Office concluded that 54 percent of a sample of CDBG projects it surveyed were so minor that they could be expected to have little if any impact on the environment. [5] In projects with an environmental impact, several critics, furthermore, raised concerns about the capacity of local governments to handle the environmental review. [6] The General Accounting Office survey confirmed their fears, concluding that some communities were "not effectively carrying out [their] environmental responsibilities." [7] In Norwich, for example, the failure of city officials to consider the historic value of the Falls site led both to long delays and to changes in the project plans.

The environmental review requirements were the most troublesome but were not the only HUD requirements. By law, HUD also demanded a set of plans from each city—affirmative action, citizen participation, fair housing. These plans proved not nearly as problematic but as one Bridgeport administrator complained, "It eats up a lot of staff time—it takes us away from other activities."

FROM PLANS TO ACTION

Despite these problems—problems that all cities and projects shared—CDBG projects in the four cities showed a remarkable range of outcomes. What elements accounted for these differences in the ability of local governments to transform plans into action? Three factors were crucial: political leadership, citizen support, and bureaucratic expertise.

Political Leadership

The leadership of elected officials played a crucial role in moving projects from plans to action. The term itself defies easy definition but we will here consider two manifestations: the support of elected officials for particular projects and the ability of elected officials to mediate conflicts among opposing factions on a project.

Project support. Martha Derthick has illustrated the role of aggressive project support by Lyndon Johnson in his New Towns program.[8] Johnson's concentrated attention in the first phase of the program brought different parts of the federal bureaucracy together to develop a quick plan to meet his goals transforming vacant federally owned land in metropolitan areas into housing for the poor. Later, when Vietnam diverted his attention from the program, enthusiasm among administrators waned and implementation slowed.[9]

Similarly, the exercise of political leadership by elected officials in the cities contributed to the implementation of several projects. In New Haven, Logue's continued insistence that the Redevelopment Agency produce a Neighborhood Preservation Plan forced the agency to change its work priorities. Logue eventually got the preservation plan—perhaps in a less ambitious form than he might have preferred and certainly after a far longer wait than he intended. Nevertheless, he succeeded in getting a plan from agency officials who clearly had other projects on which they would rather have spent their time. In Bridgeport, Mandanici's constant questions on the status of the Waterfront Park Project kept ODA staff members working to resolve the complexities of the project.

All officials—elected or appointed—faced many strong and competing demands on their time and expertise. Elected officials forced quicker movement in some projects than others by setting priorities for administrative action. In some cases, like Neighborhood Preservation, this priority setting was direct: the mayor ordered the redevelopment agency to develop a plan. In other cases, like the Waterfront Park Project, this priority setting was more subtle and indirect: the mayor directed a stream of requests for status reports. The New London city council similarly made the Bank Street Project the center of local attention by spending considerable time reviewing project plans and listening to citizens' views.

In both cases, the concentration of elected officials on a particular project influenced the amount of time administrators spent on it and hence the progress the administrators made toward implementation. Elected officials, however, also faced serious constraints on their time and energy as well. They could exert such leadership on only a handful of projects. The tool thus was quite limited in scope if powerful in application.

Conflict mediation. In addition to forcing concentrated administrative attention to projects, elected officials also at times developed compromises among disputing parties. The city council and administrative officials in New London, for example, worked out a successful Bank Street agreement between the merchants (who favored demolition of deteriorating buildings) and the historic preservation forces (who demanded that the buildings be saved). The compromise won the support of the merchants, eliminated the possibility that the historic preservation forces would sue to block the project, and eased the way to implementation.

The failure of elected officials to play a mediating role, furthermore, sometimes created roadblocks to projects. The reluctance of New London council members to develop a compromise site for the new fire station led to no fire station at all. In Norwich, as the majority of the city council waited for both sides of the Rose Tower controversy to reconcile, the developer abandoned the project. Elected officials were often in a position to intervene between contesting factions. But for the same reasons they chose to avoid conflict in budgeting, they rarely found it in their interest to expose themselves in disputes over implementation.

Citizen Support

Project implementation could, of course, succeed without citizen involvement. The sparse writings on implementation, in fact, make scant mention of individual citizens' roles in the process. Yet the suggestions and support of citizens improved the content and pace of the implementation of some CDBG projects while citizen opposition destroyed others. The role of citizens in the CDBG projects was particularly important when planners designed the projects and then moved to fulfill them.

Project design. New London's Bank Street proposal stimulated an enormous amount of public debate through the city council meetings, Citizen Advisory Council sessions, public hearings, and the newspapers. The arguments were complex and sometimes heated. Should the city tear down some of the older buildings? Should the city provide more downtown parking? How about a boardwalk? The answers that emerged from these questions—and from the arguments that followed—improved the project, most contestants agreed. The plan would revitalize the downtown business district (as the merchants wanted) while saving the city's historic spirit (as the historic preservation forces demanded). And many more residents returned to the downtown area to stroll, shop, and dine.

In Bridgeport's Park Improvement Project, the Citizens Union selected the sites for new park projects. Although their involvement led to the scattering that the critics condemned, the citizen role not only broadened the political acceptability of the Park Improvement Project in particular but also of the city's CDBG program in general. In Norwich, on the other hand, citizen opposition to the downtown site for Rose Tower effectively killed the project.

Plan fulfillment. The importance of citizen political involvement continued as administrators moved from design to fulfillment of project plans. Citizen support eased the way for New London's Bank Street Project and Bridgeport's Park Improvement Project. Citizen opposition hindered Bridgeport's ODA in implementing the Waterfront Project and blocked New London's fire station.

Citizen involvement, however, went past demonstrations of public opinion. In New Haven, neighborhood residents played an active role in administering the Neighborhood Preservation Project. Residents in each neighborhood surveyed housing conditions and selected target streets. Their role served several purposes. First, having citizens make the choices relieved city officials of the burden of excluding some streets from the project. Second, the choice of target streets by citizens (based on their own perceptions and knowledge of their neighborhood) eliminated the need for city officials to develop "objective" criteria for making choices over alternatives where none was demonstrably "best." Third, having citizens make the choices strengthened public support for the project and improved communication between city hall and the neighborhoods.

Not all local administrators, naturally, felt kindly toward a strong citizen role, for effective citizen participation often came at the expense of bureaucratic discretion. Providing an opportunity for citizen participation, furthermore, often itself brought delays. One Bridgeport official complained, "This is democracy—what can I say? If you give everybody the opportunity to say their two cents, this is what you get." The citizens nevertheless added an important element to the implementation of many CDBG projects.

Bureaucratic Effectiveness

No matter how strong the support from politicians and citizens for a project, no project succeeded unless the administering agency had the capacity to deal with the project's complexities. Two kinds of complexity were important for the CDBG projects: the complexity of dealing with the intricacies of each project; and the complexity of working with other participants in the intergovernmental system.

Project complexity. Some of the projects were administratively simple. Implementing Bridgeport's Park Improvement Project, for example, was a relatively straightforward matter of drawing up specifications, soliciting bids, and letting contracts according to established city procedures. Other projects, however, were far more complex. New Haven's Neighborhood Preservation Project, for example, involved an intricate series of steps: deciding on a general strategy; developing a formula for allocating the funds among the neighborhoods and their residents; choosing target streets; encouraging eligible residents to apply; and establishing a new agency to administer the project. Yet New Haven did it—as did New London in the Bank Street Project—and began work on fulfilling the plans.

Neither Bridgeport's Waterfront Project nor Norwich's Falls Project fared so well. Both were elaborate projects in areas where the administering agencies had no previous experience. The Waterfront Park Project snagged on ODA's excessive ambition: ODA had developed imaginative plans without a corresponding capability to carry them out. The Falls Project foundered for months as city officials changed the project from total clearance to a less ambitious plan combining road improvements with housing rehabilitation. City officials were still struggling with the development of detailed plans when they encountered the historic preservation problem.

Each city's success in dealing with project complexity was inseparably bound with its previous experience. The more experienced cities kept to projects within the bounds of their administrative capacity. In part, this was because their experience had developed administrative strength over the years. They had staffs with the expertise and established procedures to deal with complicated projects. In part, this was also because they had developed a better sense of which project to avoid. The less experienced cities, on the other hand, developed projects that lay beyond their capacity. Not only did they struggle with the intricacies of the projects themselves, but they also had to train staff and develop procedures for resolving those complexities. The dual problem created further delays. [10]

System complexity. Some of the projects, furthermore, extensively involved participants from other levels of government. Sometimes the intergovernmental involvement came through complex financial arrangements where the cities tried to combine their CDBG funds with other federal money. Both New Haven's Taft Project and Norwich's Rose Tower Project, for example, required Section 8 subsidies (a program administered independently of the CDBG program). Bridgeport officials relied on federal Bureau of Outdoor Recreation funds administered by the Connecticut State Department of Environmental Protection for their Waterfront Park

Project. Sometimes the intergovernmental involvement came through regulation. Federal historic preservation officials blocked Norwich's Falls Project and Bridgeport officials needed a collection of state and federal permits for their Waterfront Park Project.

Each concurrence required from a different level of government caused delay,[11] not only because of the time needed to solicit a separate approval but also because each new approval required the project to meet a new set of goals. Winning approval from other governmental levels always caused delays, sometimes demanded changes in project plans, and occasionally scuttled the projects altogether. None of the projects that significantly involved other governmental levels were very successful.*

IMPLICATIONS FOR PROJECT EXECUTION

The Rocky Road to Success

How do these three factors—political leadership, citizen support, and bureaucratic effectiveness—apply to the execution of the projects examined in the case studies? Table 6.1 arrays the factors influencing the " success" or "failure" of the projects as measured by how closely the results matched their original plans. These factors point to important differences between the best- and worst-case projects.

The best-case projects, on the whole, had the strong backing of elected officials, support of (or at least the absence of opposition from) citizens, and an administering agency with the expertise to deal with the project's complexity. No one factor proved a determinant of success. Of the best-case projects, Neighborhood Preservation in New Haven and Bank Street in New London received support from all three factors. Bridgeport's Park Improvement Project, however, had no strong political leadership behind it, and Norwich's Falls Project aroused little public interest.

Bureaucratic effectiveness, however, was a precondition for executing each project. The point is simple: without sufficient administrative competence it was impossible to tend to the details of a project no matter how much political leadership and citizen support lay behind the project. And indeed, Norwich's Falls Project

_____

*These projects were New Haven's Taft Project; Bridgeport's Waterfront Park Project; and Norwich's two projects, the Falls Project and the Rose Tower Project.

demonstrates just this. The project had the full backing of city officials yet project administrators could not negotiate the rocky road
to completion and completed little of the project. (It is worth re-
membering that the project was a "best case" relative to other Norwich CDBG projects, not compared with the projects in other cities.)

TABLE 6.1

Factors Influencing Project Execution
(Factors contributing to "success" (+) or "failure" (-);
0 indicates no significant role in project.)

	Political Leadership	Citizen Support	Bureaucratic Effectiveness
Bridgeport			
Best case: parks	0	+	+
Worst case: waterfront	+	-	-
New Haven			
Best case: preservation	+	+	+
Worst case: Taft	+	0	-
New London			
Best case: Bank Street	+	+	+
Worst case: fire station	0	-	0
Norwich			
Best case: Falls	+	0	-
Worst case: Rose Tower	0	-	-

But bureaucratic skill alone was not enough. Administrators
set to work on none of the projects in a vacuum; there were always
other demands on their time and always more things that could be
done than there was time in which to do them. Attention by other
officials or by citizens to a project determined in part which projects received the administrators' highest priority. Hence, political
leadership and citizen support influenced the focus of an administering agency's skills.

Furthermore, issues in execution were rarely purely technical and often were intensely political: for example, which houses
would be rehabilitated, which streets would receive help first, what
income standards would determine which families could receive

assistance, and so on. It is hard to imagine a purely rational or value-free solution to these puzzles, and even if there were such a solution it might engender so much opposition as to stop the project. Political leadership and citizen support thus complemented administrative effectiveness in two ways: they helped produce solutions for thorny administrative questions, and they provided a political base of support on which project execution proceeded.

The worst-case projects lagged behind the best cases because of two problems. First, administrators could not tackle the technical details of the projects (in three of the four projects). Second, the project lacked either political leadership from elected officials or support from the citizens (in three out of the four cases). The relative success or failure of the projects thus hinged on the interplay of administrative and political factors.

The Variety of Local Outcomes

Although project execution did not vary by the size of the city, the outcomes did vary by the city's previous experience with similar programs. While elected officials in the more experienced cities were relatively successful in executing their key projects (like New Haven's Hotel Taft and New London's Bank Street projects), the lack of success in key projects frustrated officials in the less-experienced cities. Officials in the less-experienced cities were particularly frustrated because the worst-case projects had been designed as the cornerstone of each city's CDBG program. Bridgeport's Waterfront Park Project was to be the centerpiece of the city's renewed downtown, and Norwich's Rose Tower Project was to reverse the crawl of blight across the central business district. In the more experienced cities, officials moved their key projects, sometimes slowly, toward completion. In the less-experienced cities, however, officials sometimes found it difficult even to begin.

Part of the explanation is the obvious one: that the cities carried their previous experience over to CDBG. This expertise was particularly concentrated in the redevelopment agencies. New Haven placed its Neighborhood Preservation Project in its Redevelopment Agency, which had conducted a large and successful Section 312 housing rehabilitation program for years. The New London Redevelopment Agency applied many of the same skills it used in creating a downtown mall to the Bank Street Project. Bridgeport and Norwich did not have equivalent experience. The greater experience in New Haven and New London did not guarantee success, but it did provide an essential first ingredient for executing CDBG projects.

Their experience particularly paid off in designing projects that lay within their expertise. Bridgeport's Waterfront Park and Norwich's Falls Project were ambitious designs. The plans not only outstripped the local governments' abilities to execute them, but they also drew agencies from other levels of government deeply into the process. This involvement of other levels expanded the number of clearances required to complete the projects, and, at the minimum, delayed the execution of projects. Because of their dearth of experience, the less-experienced cities faced a large array of unanticipated entanglements that the more experienced cities avoided. [12]

EFFECTIVENESS, EXPERTISE, AND CONTROL

Controlling the Experts

Among the political and administrative factors influencing the execution of CDBG projects is a hidden problem. The more-experienced cities did not necessarily have a consistently easier time in executing their projects, for with greater bureaucratic expertise came a greater problem in controlling the experts. Each city, in fact, struggled with a trade-off: marshaling sufficient administrative expertise to implement the projects effectively while keeping that expertise under the control of elected officials and their constituents.

Years of experience had built the redevelopment agencies in the cities into the prime source of local expertise. Although, as we have noted, the level of expertise varied by city, redevelopment officials had resources no one else in their town could match. They had friends in HUD who could explain the workings of the program. They had established procedures to deal with recurring tasks. They had planners familiar with local problems, and they had more of the planners than any other city agency. As one New Haven Redevelopment Agency official explained:

> Fortunately or unfortunately, [the program] is very complex and it takes [the mayor] a while to catch on— the sophisticated nuances of this program which can save you half a million bucks if you write it this way or blow the whole deal if you put it that way are not readily available to everyone.

Perhaps most important of all, the years of HUD's urban renewal program built into the redevelopment agencies a narrow sense of their mission and a strong sense of their own independence. They existed to rebuild the city. They did so—or tried to do so—with a pride that grew into an agency ethos. And they did so—especially in the later years—relatively free from the constraints of the local political process.*

With the CDBG program, however, the redevelopment agencies lost control over both their budgets and the scope of their projects. New Haven Mayor Frank Logue charged the agency with developing a rehabilitation plan. New London's city council asked the agency to rehabilitate a downtown street. In both cases, elected officials encountered resistance. Logue waited months for the project plans; New London council members faced delays as the Redevelopment Agency's board insisted on approving the details of the project. In both cases, it was because the rehabilitation approach conflicted with the established goals and procedures of the agencies. Redevelopment people "have some ingrained approaches," Logue discovered. A consultant to several cities in the program said, "It is very difficult for the redevelopment process to be unseated."

The less-experienced cities set out to avoid the control problem by establishing new centralized agencies under the direct control of elected officials.[13] In both Bridgeport and Norwich, elected officials subordinated the redevelopment agencies to new community development bureaus. Redevelopment agency officials clearly understood the message and resigned themselves to eventual organizational death.[14] But a Norwich agency official complained: "You've got a staff of people [in the Redevelopment Agency] who know the program. [Instead], you set up an agency to do the same thing but staff it with people who don't know the program . . ., who aren't sure what they want to do." The new community development bureaus began from scratch. They had to hire a staff and develop procedures (like processing contracts) before they could even begin the work of implementing projects. Elected officials achieved control at the expense of existing expertise.

There were many officials in the less-experienced cities who felt that the advantages of increased control more than compensated for the loss of expertise. Similarly, officials in the more active cities accepted—somewhat reluctantly—the stubbornness of existing agencies in return for their skills.

---

*Richard C. Lee's leadership of urban renewal in New Haven is a notable exception. Lee succeeded in motivating the local political system in support of redevelopment. In the later years of his tenure, however, the Redevelopment Agency's independence grew. That independence blossomed under Lee's successor, Bart Guida.

What factors determined this set of balances in the expertise-control trade-off? The more experienced cities had redevelopment agencies with greater expertise; they stood to lose that expertise if they established new agencies. Furthermore, the agencies themselves had built political strength over the years and would have strongly resisted any attempt to dismantle them. In the less-experienced cities, on the other hand, the redevelopment agencies had less power to resist takeover.

Importing Expertise

The expertise problem also varied with the size of the city. The larger cities—Bridgeport and New Haven—had both sufficiently large entitlements and reasonable expectations of continued federal support to justify a fully staffed CDBG agency. For the smaller cities—New London and Norwich—the situation was different. Although New London had a very large entitlement for a city of its size, city officials expected the grant amount to shrink or perhaps disappear within a few years. Norwich officials not only shared this concern but also had a much smaller entitlement. Local officials in the smaller cities, therefore, were reluctant to take on the maintenance costs of a large staff. Both cities established only a four-member CDBG staff.

The program, however, imposed a set of administrative burdens on all recipients regardless of the size of their entitlements or the number of their projects. These burdens—program compliance, planning, contracting, monitoring—were beyond the capacity of a four-member staff. From the very beginning of the program, New London solved the problem by importing expertise: hiring consultants from outside the city's government to perform general planning, environmental reviews, and evaluation of public services. As Norwich officials encountered problems in their projects, they increasingly relied on consultants.

The role of outside experts in the smaller cities was ironic. The CDBG program had as one of its subsidiary goals the development of local administrative capacity. But when they faced administrative problems, the smaller cities sought outside help instead of building internal capacity. The unstable nature of the program and the pressures of the local political system discouraged any attempt to strengthen the cities' abilities to handle future problems.

Managing Local Development

The failure of CDBG decision makers to consider questions of execution in the budgetary process produced the central pathology of the execution process: delay. The amount of money that city officials budgeted for projects usually indicated only their political priority, not how much it would cost to complete the project. In fact, as one official pointed out, city officials rarely knew what they wanted done. Execution stopped às elected officials and administrators developed project details. These delays occasionally became fatal as officials realized that they had chosen unimplementable projects. Delays also occurred as city officials developed management systems for the program and as they struggled to meet HUD's requirements.

Not all delays had a negative impact on implementation. Sometimes the delays produced strong leadership from elected officials. Conflict among community factions that differed over details of a project often ended both in improvements to the project and in a broader base of public support for it. But sometimes the lack of political leadership by elected officials combined with citizen opposition to kill a project.

All four cities faced similar problems yet the cities produced widely different outcomes. Of all the factors that contributed to these differences, the most important was bureaucratic effectiveness. It was the precondition without which execution proceeded haltingly. And it was the factor that produced greater success in the more-experienced cities as they executed their projects.

This is a conclusion with uncomfortable implications for vesting cities with broader intergovernmental responsibilities. It suggests that experience is indeed the best teacher and that structural change alone is inadequate to improve local management capacity. In fact, both cities that undertook substantial reorganizations suffered delays as the new agencies geared up to meet the CDBG program's challenges. Administrative capacity does not easily flow from structural change and cannot be simply transferred. It is, rather, part of a slow learning process.

Learning for the cities is always a slow and often an uneven process. Some cities begin with more experience and more experts and can progress more quickly. Other cities begin from scratch and take longer to acquire knowledge. There is no simple shortcut to the learning process, and since cities learn at different rates they are likely to reach different levels of administrative capacity. Hence, no uniform assumptions about local capacity seem safe unless they are the most conservative.

Complicating the learning problem for cities was the constant change of subject matter. Cities in the 1960s and 1970s watched a steady parade of federal programs come and go, each with its own goals, rules, and demands. Some programs, like the antipoverty programs, sought to weaken city hall and strengthen the neighborhoods.

Others, like urban renewal, strengthened administrative officials at the expense of elected officials. CDBG attempted to centralize power in the hands of elected officials. The stream of changes discouraged attempts by cities to build administrative capacity for they could only guess at what kind of expertise they would need next.

Nevertheless, the parade of federal programs has been an important force behind the gradual growth of local expertise. In all four cities the federal grants have induced local governments to establish new agencies with new technical capabilities. The grants have taken local governments into new functional areas like downtown economic development and the rehabilitation of private housing. The grants have also produced new management techniques like the use of contracts to specify and measure performance.

In the end, however, nearly everyone in the cities placed far more emphasis on the distribution of CDBG funds than on what the money would accomplish. It was the symbolic value of the projects and the actual flow of cash that were the central points of political interest. The bargaining process that resulted may have produced a politically satisfactory budget but it left the local CDBG program essentially leaderless. And without a strong central leader the problem of controlling the administrative experts—whose subjugation to elected officials, of course, was one of the prime goals of the CDBG program—became even more difficult.

NOTES

1. Eugene Bardach similarly sees delay as the central problem of implementation. See The Implementation Game: What Happens after a Bill Becomes a Law (Cambridge, Mass.: MIT Press, 1977), p. 180.

2. The concern by elected officials for inputs over outputs, Lyle C. Fitch argues, plagues local governments in general. See his testimony, U.S. Congress, House, Committee on Banking and Currency, Housing and Urban Development Legislation—1971, hearings before the Subcommittee on Housing, 92nd Cong., 1st sess., 1971, pp. 585-86.

3. Hugh Heclo, A Government of Strangers: Executive Politics in Washington (Washington, D.C.: Brookings, 1977), p. 179. Other students of bureaucratic politics have made similar observations. See Morton H. Halperin and Arnold Kanter's "Introduction" to their edited collection, Readings in American Foreign Policy: A Bureaucratic Perspective (Boston: Little, Brown, 1973), p. 34; Walter Williams, "Implementation Analysis and Assessment," in Social Program Implementation, ed. Walter Williams and Richard

F. Elmore (New York: Academic Press, 1976), p. 270; and Bardach, The Implementation Game, p. 90.

4. Eugene Bardach and Lucian Pugliaresi, "The Environmental Impact Statement vs. the Real World," The Public Interest no. 49 (Fall 1977): 22–38, esp. p. 36.

5. U.S. General Accounting Office, Environmental Reviews Done by Communities: Are They Needed? Are They Adequate? (September 1, 1977), p. 7. See also U.S. Congress, House, Committee on Banking, Finance and Urban Affairs, Community Development Block Grant Program, report by the staff of the Subcommittee on Housing and Community Development, Committee Print, 95th Cong., 1st sess., February 1977, p. 57.

6. U.S. General Accounting Office, Environmental Reviews, p. 3.

7. Ibid., p. ii.

8. Martha Derthick, New Towns In-Town (Washington, D.C.: The Urban Institute, 1972).

9. Ibid., p. 83. The basic cause of the "failure" of the program, however, lay deeper than the loss of presidential leadership. Derthick contends the major problems were "the limited ability of the federal government to influence the actions of local governments" and the federal government's "tendency to conceive goals in ideal terms."

10. In a study of Title I of the Elementary and Secondary Education Act, Stephen K. Bailey and Edith K. Mosher predicted that the lack of local administrative expertise would plague block grants. See ESEA: The Office of Education Administers a Law (Syracuse, N.Y.: Syracuse University Press, 1968), pp. 216-17.

11. This point is best put by Jeffrey L. Pressman and Aaron Wildavsky's discussion of "the complexity of joint action." See Implementation (Berkeley: University of California Press, 1973), pp. 87-124. For a similar argument, see Robert A. Levine, Public Planning: Failure and Redirection (New York: Basic Books, 1972), p. 138.

12. Despite the volume of studies on the CDBG program, few reports have examined the administration of the program. Two studies, however, have reached important conclusions. The report prepared by the staff of the House Subcommittee on Housing and Community Development of the Committee on Banking, Finance and Urban Affairs concluded that cities with previous categorical grant experience produced dramatic results more quickly than cities without experience (Community Development Block Grant Program, p. 49). Although the subcommittee staff made distinctions only between cities with some experience and cities with no experience,

their conclusions are suggestive of the relationship between experience and performance.

The Southern Regional Council's study also looked briefly at the problem of administrative capacity. They concluded that "many jurisdictions presently lack the administrative and planning capacity to carry out the complex . . . procedures that are vital to the effective delivery of services to low- and moderate-income persons." See Raymond Brown with Ann Coil and Carol Rose, A Time for Accounting: The Housing and Community Development Act in the South (Atlanta: Southern Regional Council, March 1976), pp. 109-10.

13. For a discussion of administrative reorganization as a strategy of control, see Herbert Kaufman, The Limits of Organizational Change (University: University of Alabama Press, 1971), p. 54; and Levine, Public Planning, p. 160.

14. Herbert Kaufman described this as the "selecting-out" of rigid organizations for extermination. See Are Government Organizations Immortal? (Washington, D.C.: Brookings, 1976), p. 69.

7
DECENTRALIZATION AND URBAN POLICY

THE FRUITS OF LOCAL DISCRETION

Local Performance

The CDBG program placed the burden for effective performance squarely on the cities. Which projects the program funded
depended on which projects the cities chose. How successful those
projects were hinged on how well the cities could muster the resources needed to fulfill the plans. Gone were the nooks and cran-
nies of categorical regulations in which local officials could hide.
CDBG exposed local officials—particularly mayors and council members—to full scrutiny. The success of local CDBG programs ulti-
mately depended on their performance.

The program thus established a far different role, compared
with the preceding programs, for the cities in the intergovernmental
system. The cities became executors of their own policies rather
than agents of a policy determined in Washington. The federal government, of course, followed the cities' performances closely and,
as we saw in Chapter 2, increasingly tightened their grip on local
behavior. But national urban policy, to the extent there was one,
was no more than the accumulated decisions and administrative actions of the country's local governments.

In the four cities we have examined, the outcomes varied widely. The cities spent their money on a broad collection of projects
and produced results ranging from lively success to outright failure.
This wide variety was especially remarkable because the cities were
all within the same state, all worked under the jurisdiction of the
same HUD area office, suffered essentially the same urban problems, and worked within the same federal program.

Nevertheless, the cities shared common features. Budgeting was bargaining, and the participants in the bargaining process were interests ranging from neighborhood-based organizations to city administrators to elected officials. Comprehensive, planned strategies existed only in the imaginations of planners who sought, after the budgetary decisions were made, to write an application that would win HUD's approval. The projects that emerged from the bargaining process were characteristically scattered around the city, designed for short-term results, and concentrated on neighborhoods. Execution of the projects was varied, with success (at least in terms of the completion of the projects as planned) depending on each project's political support by city leaders and citizens and on the administering agency's capacity.

Creeping Categorization

The CDBG program produced few flashy projects that rivaled the large projects of the categoricals. In New Haven, where federal dollars had previously totally rebuilt the city's downtown, CDBG produced no project that worked as enormous a change or could so capture the imagination of planners. The program, so much greater in its variety, was also much more limited in the vision of results it could produce. Only in a few cities across the country did CDBG produce monumental change; in most cities, CDBG produced small groups of rehabilitated homes, new trees along streets, expanded social services, and improved parks. In a search for clear results, the program produced few gripping symbols. As a result, it was hard for the program's proponents to point to obvious benefits flowing from the cities' exercise of discretion. And if the cities could not produce results—or if their results were not plainly visible—some critics argued that the money ought to be placed back in federal hands.

The lack of clear symbols for the program's benefits combined with two other problems on the road to retrenchment: an incessant need for definition by HUD of the program's details and stories of local governments' abuse of the program.

The program as enacted by Congress contained a great deal of unclear and ambiguous language. In releasing its first regulations on the program, HUD, trying to act in the spirit of the New Federalism, used most of the act's language. A host of questions predictably arose. How thoroughly should HUD's area offices review local applications? Was the purchase of Little League baseball uniforms an eligible expenditure? What did "maximum feasible priority" of the needs of the poor mean? The result was a spate of "Meeker

Memos" from Assistant Secretary David O. Meeker, Jr. (as described in Chapter 2) that numbered more than 100 before the program's first anniversary. The questions also led to more than 100 pages of regulations in the Federal Register during the program's first two years. Each new Meeker Memo or regulation had a dual effect: it increased the red tape associated with the program, and it drew at least a small measure of discretion back to HUD from the cities.

Furthermore, as the cities began to budget their money, the results disturbed many Washington-based interest groups, especially those representing minorities and the poor. Although the program had several goals, these interest groups concentrated (not surprisingly) on the program's impact on minorities and the poor. As we saw in Chapter 2, they did not like what they discovered. With the program's projects scattered around the cities, these groups were not the chief beneficiaries of the program, certainly compared with Model Cities and other categorical programs. These interest groups produced tales of program abuse like construction of tennis courts, marinas, and country club improvements. Some of these tales were truly cases of abuse, but most were projects defensible by other program goals. These horror stories, however, created substantial adverse publicity for CDBG and brought demands for greater supervision by HUD of the cities' decisions.

In addition to the horror stories, there were undoubtedly also logistical reasons behind the interest groups' demands. The principal intergovernmental lobbies for the poor, like the NAACP and the Urban League, were staffed to fight limited, concentrated battles, principally of course in Washington. CDBG made it impossible for these interest groups to influence the allocation of funds since the decisions were being made in thousands of cities across the country. Greater HUD supervision would mean more centralization of power and thus a greater chance of influencing key decisions. The two factors combined to produce demands for recentralization of community development policy in Washington.

The interest groups' work led to tough questioning of HUD officials by members of the key congressional oversight committees. The committees were interested in reports, particularly from the National Association of Housing and Redevelopment Officials, that less than half of the CDBG money was going to low- and moderate-income neighborhoods. HUD began paying greater attention to the income of neighborhoods in which the cities located projects. HUD increasingly forced the cities to identify the beneficiaries of the projects and to make sure that the poor received a larger share of the benefits. Patricia Harris, Jimmy Carter's first HUD secretary, intensified this effort as soon as she took office.

The result was a set of new regulations, more attention by HUD to local applications and less discretion for the cities in how to spend the money. Slowly, the same disease that had afflicted other block grant programs attacked CDBG: "creeping categorization," a term coined by the U.S. Advisory Commission on Intergovernmental Relations (ACIR) to describe the efforts of federal grant agencies, interest groups, and congressional committees to concentrate the attention of state and local governments on specific national priorities.[1] In a survey of four block grant programs—Partnership for Health, Safe Streets, Comprehensive Employment and Training (CETA), and CDBG—the ACIR found creeping categorization to be part of the aging process of block grants.* As each of the grants aged, they became more encumbered with regulations imposed by both Congress and the administering agencies, regulations that increasingly sought national objectives at the expense of state and local discretion.

The roots of creeping categorization—and even more important shifts in federal-local relations—lay in two problems. First, the program overloaded both the political and administrative capacity of the cities. This overload produced problems that resulted in demands for more federal power and less local discretion.[2] Second, federal and local officials saw the program much differently. As local officials pursued different goals than federal officials intended, the federal officials tightened the reins on local governments. The result of these two features has been but part of larger, important changes in the intergovernmental system.

OVERLOADING THE CITIES

Political Overload

CDBG stimulated huge new demands for federal money. The program's advance advertising was as a no-strings revenue sharing program, and this created a grab-bag mentality from which CDBG never advanced. Local interests from city agencies to neighborhood-based organizations saw CDBG as "new" money that could be spent on nearly anything. Local officials, especially in the first years of the program, were deluged with far more demands for projects than local officials could hope to satisfy.

---

*ACIR did not study the fifth block grant, the Title XX amendments to the Social Security Act (enacted in 1974).

But even after the program began to settle into a more regular pattern, local officials continued to find themselves besieged by groups seeking money. Despite HUD's increasing regulation of the program, local officials still had far broader discretion in how to use the money than they did in the categoricals. They could decide which functional areas would receive how much money, which geographical areas would receive the most attention, and in the end, which projects would be funded. This discretion, despite its obvious advantages for local officials, posed a large problem: it robbed local officials of the protection of federal regulations. No longer could they say, "We have to do it this way because the feds make us" or "Your part of the city cannot be included because of federal regulations." The program clearly focused the responsibility for these hard choices on local elected officials.

As we saw in Chapter 5, local elected officials shrank from these decisions in a pattern of avoiding conflict where possible. Instead, an unstructured bargaining process among local combatants, what Douglas Yates has called "street-fighting pluralism," determined how the money would be spent. [3]

CDBG overloaded the local political process by creating large demands, by supplying resources inadequate to fill those demands, and by denying local officials any defense behind federal regulations. This political overload made budgeting by bargaining inevitable.

Administrative Overload

The sudden influx of CDBG money seriously challenged local administrative machinery. The problem was not only the large size of the grant relative to the municipal budget, for large amounts of money had been flowing to the cities from the federal government for years. Earlier programs had channeled federal money to Model Cities organizations, to urban renewal agencies, to sewer authorities. For the first time in CDBG, however, federal community development dollars were flowing into a single receptacle, city hall, which faced the task of managing the cash.

Few organizations, at any level of government or in the private sector, would find it easy to deal with such a rapid increase in responsibility. Leaving aside the problem of how to spend the money, which we have examined in the political side of the overload question, CDBG brought problems of controlling the money: defining contract terms, writing contracts, distributing and accounting for the money, monitoring the use of the money, and keeping records to comply with general federal requirements, among many other tasks. The growth problem alone—dealing with the increase in money to be managed—would have presented a formidable challenge. But CDBG also presented two other challenges: expansion into relatively new (for city governments) functional areas; and the acquisition of skilled staff to handle the problems.

The staffing problem was especially difficult. Most of the community development expertise in the cities rested with the urban renewal agencies yet the program explicitly sought to weaken the administrators of the former categorical programs. Elected officials had two choices. They could rely on the expertise of the administrators and sacrifice some of their own control or they could hire new staffs and sacrifice the administrators' know-how. Bridgeport, New London, and Norwich elected to build new staffs; New Haven relied on the redevelopment agency. Each city initially suffered the predictable consequences of the path they had chosen, but as the program developed, the administrative relationships settled into a more stable pattern. Community development agencies in the first three cities gradually became more competent, and in New Haven the mayor learned better how to deal with the redevelopment agency.

These relationships were crucial because, with the change in community development grants from categorical to block, the cities lost an important administrative aid. For all of the problems with federal review of local grant applications (chronicled in Chapter 1), the review provided at least a thorough examination of the steps toward execution of local projects. The long delays in application processing, in fact, were due to step-by-step review of local plans. The projects were not guaranteed successful execution once approved. But the federal application reviews did at least guarantee that execution problems would be examined before funds were committed. In CDBG, however, even devising the plans for the execution of projects—without considering their feasibility—usually did not occur until after the cities had budgeted their money. CDBG succeeded merely in shifting the delay from the federal application review to the local postbudgeting planning. And at least in the beginning of the program, the hands doing this planning were relatively inexperienced.

For local officials, these administrative chores were imposing. Each city funded many projects, sometimes over 100 in each year, and administrators had to supervise and account for each project. In addition, the program carried with it a set of general grant requirements—from nondiscrimination to environmental protection—that for the first time were a local responsibility. Because of HUD's principle of supporting local discretion, the agency gave little technical assistance. Building local administrative strength to meet these needs was a slow and uneasy process.

Making things more difficult for the cities were the constant regulation changes. Local officials complained that just as they mastered one set of regulations, HUD would issue a new rule. In trying to meet HUD's regulations, the cities were aiming at a moving target. The ACIR discovered that this was a problem that extended across the entire intergovernmental grant system.[4] In the CDBG program, these changes made the program unpredictable and hence even more difficult to manage.

All of these factors combined to create an administrative overload on the cities. The cities were suddenly confronted by new and significant administrative responsibilities that lay beyond their capacity. They responded slowly by reorganizing their community development agencies, by hiring new staff, and by creating new procedures to handle the new problems. But this learning process inevitably created delays in executing projects, and the delays in turn created the impression that the cities could not handle their new responsibilities. It is at least debatable whether other organizations—notably the federal government—could have achieved results any quicker, given such massive changes in administrative arrangements. The cities' struggles during their learning period, however, gave added support to critics who sought to return power to the federal government.

THE FEDERAL-LOCAL RELATIONSHIP

CDBG significantly affected both the allocation of federal money and the character of federal-local relations. As we saw in Chapter 4, the cities pursued a basically distributive approach in allocating their money, compared with the more narrowly focused redistributive approach of the categoricals. In addition, as we saw in Chapter 2, the federal-local relationship also changed: in CDBG, with nearly automatic entitlement of local governments to the money, the federal government played an increasingly regulative role. These two changes—distributive politics at the local level coupled with regulative politics at the intergovernmental level—produced some interesting implications for the future balance of power between the federal government and the cities.

This balance of power problem rests on two separate questions that return us to the double dilemma presented in Chapter 1. First, who should decide the allocation of national resources? How can we balance our pursuit of national goals, our reverence for local self-determination, and our worries about democracy in American cities? Second, once we set this political balance, how can we administer it?

The Allocation of Federal Money

Economists have traditionally argued, as we saw in Chapter 1, that redistribution of the nation's income to address the needs of the poor is properly the function of the national government. Not only do local governments usually lack the resources to engage in redistribution, but any locally undertaken redistribution would only encourage the concentration of the poor and thus further increase the local financial burden. Furthermore, any benefits that resulted from local actions would spill over into surrounding areas while the costs would be borne by the local government itself. Thus, the argument goes, the primary responsibility for redistribution rests with the federal government. [5]

At least since the Depression, the federal government has pursued this policy in its grants to local governments. Washington has borne more than two-thirds of the cost of the major redistributive functions—welfare, health, housing, and social insurance[6]—and has used the intergovernmental grant as its prime distributional mechanism. Nowhere has this been more true than in community development. Beginning with the Housing Act of 1949, the federal government has struggled to improve the housing and living standards of the nation's poor. As the programs evolved through the 1960s, with urban renewal and Model Cities, federal programs remained focused on the plight of the impoverished.

CDBG continued in this tradition with its emphasis on the needs of low- and moderate-income individuals. The program also established two other goals as equal, however: the elimination of slums and blight and urgent community development needs. These goals gave the cities license to attack nearly any important city development problem, whether the problems affected the poor or not. The cities took advantage of this latitude to do just that. When this pattern caught the attention of the interest groups, however, they used the projects as evidence that the cities could not be trusted with discretion in using federal money. The poor, they claimed, would inevitably suffer.

In that the critics had a case, not so much because of malicious intent by those who ran the cities but because of the essential mechanisms of city politics. As we have seen, federal community development policy has had an essentially redistributive focus. It has tried to single out the most needy cities (although, as we saw in Chapter 1, the success of a city's application often had more to do with the skill of the writers of its grants). Within cities, it has tried to concentrate money on a narrow set of functions. But in giving CDBG to the cities, the federal government has vested substantial authority in the least redistributive level in the federal system.

Paul E. Peterson found that local governments accounted for only 7 percent of all governmental expenditures in redistributive functions (welfare, health, housing, and social insurance) in 1973. The comparable figure for state governments was 22 percent; for the federal government, 71 percent. The local share, furthermore, had declined by nearly a third from 10.8 percent in 1962.[7]

In vesting CDBG authority with the cities, Congress plunged the program into an essentially distributive environment. City governments are organizations in the business of distributing basic services: garbage collection, fire protection, road repair, and police protection. Citizens check to see if city trucks plow the snow from other neighborhoods' streets quicker from their own, if another street gets better garbage pick-up, or if their street suffers more from potholes. The most common complaints heard by mayors, a National League of Cities survey revealed, were area-specific problems about particular services: dog problems, traffic control, rezoning, potholes, sewer service, cleanliness of streets, and crime.[8] The distribution of identifiable services by identifiable areas is the key to understanding the operation and the product of local governments. The federal and state governments, of course, are also in the business of distributing services, but the cities are unique in the direct and observable links between policy decisions and the implications of those decisions for any given neighborhood. The result is that city politics is distributive politics.

City officials allocated CDBG funds the same way, although the distributional tendencies were exaggerated because there were relatively few old projects with first call on the money. Yet even as the program settled into adolescence, the basic tendency toward a broad distribution, by both function and neighborhood, remained strong.

It was the distributional politics of CDBG that was the root of the interest groups' attacks on the cities. They had supported, grown through, and benefited from the redistributive approach followed through community development's first 25 years. They argued that the cities should continue the earlier philosophy: that federal money should be concentrated on the poor. If they did not choose to do so, HUD should force them to this approach through regulations. And this was the approach HUD took as the cities on their own showed little tendency to concentrate the money on the needs of the poor.

The Drift toward Regulation

These differences between the local and the federal approach to community development led, as we have seen, to new federal regulations directing the cities to focus more of their CDBG money on the needs of low- and moderate-income families. The federal regulations, in brief, sought to force the cities from a distributive to a redistributive allocation of the money. These regulations accreted slowly in a steady drift toward regulation, a creeping backwards toward the categorical strategy of urban aid, and a movement toward new federal-local relations.

As CDBG evolved, the program increasingly resolved the double political and administrative dilemma we explored in Chapter 1 through more federal control and less local discretion. To solve the perceived problem of local program abuse, the federal government regulated in more detail how cities could spend their grants and insisted that cities demonstrate that they were meeting these rules. Some projects eligible in the program's first year became ineligible by the third. At the same time, the size of local applications doubled in a more than symbolic display of the program's increasing paperwork requirements. The cities found that the scope of their discretion had shrunk and that their administrative chores had grown. New regulations, accompanied by extensive HUD audits of local compliance with those regulations, became the primary federal administrative tool.

The program's changes, however, were not simply a move back to the categoricals. The cities still maintained substantial discretion, and the choices they enjoyed were broader than in the categoricals. The nearly automatic distribution of aid to a much larger group of cities remained as well. Missing, therefore, were key elements of the categorical strategy: federal selection of the best project proposals on the basis of competing applications.

The gradual drift in the CDBG program toward greater HUD supervision signaled more enduring changes in federal-local relations. The grant-by-formula approach, popularized by general revenue sharing and the spread of computer terminals throughout official Washington spread past CDBG into an ever-growing number of federal grant programs.[9] Federal administrative agencies have therefore been forced to redefine their roles. They spend less time deciding which projects to fund and more time insuring that state and local governments follow the rules in deciding the allocation of funds for themselves. The federal agencies, thus, have become regulators, and the federal-local relationship has become increasingly regulative.

Like CDBG, each federal program carries with it program-specific requirements. Some of these requirements specify what recipients are to do with the money: train the poor for jobs, rehabilitate homes, care for the elderly, and so on. Other requirements detail how this is to be done: what kind of planning, record-keeping, financial management, and so on. Furthermore, many general requirements applied to CDBG—particularly nondiscrimination, environmental protection, relocation, labor standards, and citizen participation, are being applied to all grant programs. Increasingly, state and local governments are principally responsible for insuring that these general requirements are met. [10]

State and local governments, instead of the federal administering agency, more and more act as the primary agents for intergovernmental policy. The federal agencies, meanwhile, assume more of an auditing role as they devise and check each program's trail of paper to insure compliance with the regulations. These compliance issues—and the regulations that define them—have grown as fundamental questions of intergovernmental relations.

DECENTRALIZATION AND THE PUBLIC INTEREST

There remains one last major question to address, and that is the one we began with: do the cities have the capacity to behave responsibly as major actors within the intergovernmental system, or to put it more simply, can the cities be trusted? As we saw in Chapters 5 and 6, conflicting answers are possible. The cities spent much of their money on important city problems but, critics complained, did not concentrate it enough. The cities executed some projects well but they either stumbled badly with or never even began other projects.

Can the cities be trusted with great discretion over large sums of money? Or does prudent management demand close federal supervision of local governments? Our examination of these four cities leads to no definitive answer.

Perhaps the better questions are: with what can the cities be trusted? And in whose interest is the decentralization of intergovernmental power? To these questions we have much clearer answers. The cities spent their money on problems that were important to those making the decisions. The process that formed those decisions, furthermore, was an unusually open one, so we can have a high degree of confidence that the cities spent their money on what they as communities saw as the most pressing problems. These projects, to be sure, tended on the whole to be relatively small and lacking in broad vision. But there was at least a reasonable defense for every project and a logic for the selection of projects that made sense within the community.

Although the execution of projects was highly uneven, many of the problems were the result of the administrative overload that the program visited upon the cities. The cities made great advances in meeting these problems as they gained more experience, but HUD made learning a frustrating, never-ending process with its constant program changes. Nevertheless, the cities were learning (although at much different rates) and, more importantly, developing the structure and resources to deal better with technical and administrative problems. This local capacity explosion, in fact, may be the most subtle yet most important result the program has produced.

CDBG as originally launched proved to be in the interest of local (principally neighborhood) goals over national goals, of local over federal officials (both elected and appointed), and of local over national interest groups. But although the program was designed to strengthen local elected officials over administrative officials at all levels, the stronger local elected officials ironically found that they needed to depend even more than ever on their administrators.

Did the cities fail, as the critics suggested? There were some problems that clearly lay beyond local capacity, particularly those that demanded long commitments (like long-term economic development), redistribution of income to the poor, or concentration of funds in a narrow functional area (like housing). The time horizon of local officials was too short and the demand for widespread distribution of benefits was too great to allow local governments to launch a concerted attack on these problems. Attacking national problems and pursuing redistribution of national income through federal grants demand greater centralization of grant strategies.

But for the many smaller-scale community development problems that plague the cities, the block grant strategy makes sense. The cities are not only capable but geared toward attacking scattered, short-term, neighborhood-based problems. There is a strong case for such a strategy in both the declining frostbelt cities, where the decay of neighborhood services only accelerates the neighborhoods' slump, and in the growing sunbelt cities, where the growth of population has often outstripped available municipal services.

The obvious strategy is a mixed set of categorical grant programs to meet long-term, redistributive problems and block grants to meet small but important problems that might otherwise fall between the cracks. But this means a readjustment of our expectation of the cities' performance, patience with cities as they learn to fulfill their expanded roles, and stabilization of urban programs so that cities, running to catch up with program changes, will at least not lose ground.

NOTES

1. U.S. Advisory Commission on Intergovernmental Relations, Summary and Concluding Observations, The Intergovernmental Grant System: An Assessment and Proposed Policies (Washington, D.C.: U.S. Government Printing Office, June 1978), p. 9.

2. For one view of the overload question, see Douglas Yates, "The Federal Government and the Urban Crisis," New York Affairs 3 (1976): 28–41.

3. Douglas Yates, The Ungovernable City: The Politics of Urban Problems and Policy Making (Cambridge, Mass.: MIT Press, 1977), pp. 33–37.

4. U.S. Advisory Commission on Intergovernmental Relations, The Intergovernmental Grant System as Seen by Local, State, and Federal Officials (Washington, D.C.: U.S. Government Printing Office, March 1977), pp. 33–44.

5. See Wallace E. Oates, "An Economist's Perspective on Fiscal Federalism," in The Political Economy of Fiscal Federalism, ed. Wallace E. Oates (Lexington, Mass.: Lexington Books, 1977), p. 5.

6. Paul E. Peterson, "The Politics of Taxation and Expenditure—A Unitary Approach." Paper prepared for presentation at the annual meeting of the American Political Science Association, New York, September 1978.

7. Ibid., p. 64.

8. Raymond L. Bancroft, "Municipal Government Today: Problems and Complaints," Nation's Cities 12 (April 1974): 16.

9. For a count of federal grant programs by type, see U.S. Advisory Commission on Intergovernmental Relations, A Catalog of Federal Grant-in-Aid Programs to State and Local Governments: Grants Funded FY 1978 (Washington, D.C.: U.S. Government Printing Office, February 1979).

10. U.S. Congressional Budget Office, Federal Constraints on State and Local Government Actions (Washington, D.C.: U.S. Government Printing Office, April 1979), esp. pp. 11–17.

BIBLIOGRAPHY

Community Development Block Grant Program

Bach, Victor. "The New Federalism in Community Development."
Social Policy 7 (January–February 1977): 32–38.

Brown, Raymond, Ann Coil, and Carol Rose. A Time for Accounting: The Housing and Community Development Act in the South.
Atlanta: Southern Regional Council, March 1976.

Center for Community Change. "Community Development Block
Grants—Implementing National Priorities." Washington, D.C.:
Center for Community Change, 1976.

Citizens Housing and Planning Council of New York, Inc. Federal
Housing Money: Making It Work in New York. New York:
Citizens Housing and Planning Council of New York, Inc., May
1976.

DeLeon, Richard, and Richard LeGates. Redistribution Effects of
Special Revenue Sharing for Community Development. Berkeley:
University of California, Berkeley, Institute of Governmental
Studies, 1976.

DeStefano, Frank, and Clay H. Wellborn. "Aspects of Community
Development Activities in Selected Localities." Washington,
D.C.: The Library of Congress Congressional Reference Ser-
vice, June 28, 1976.

Dommel, Paul R., Richard P. Nathan, Sarah F. Liebschutz,
Margaret T. Wrightson, and associates. Decentralizing Com-
munity Development. Washington, D.C.: U.S. Government
Printing Office, 1978.

Downs, Anthony, Lewis Bolan, and Margery al Chalabi. Recommendations for Community Development Planning. Chicago:
Real Estate Research Corporation, 1975.

Franklin, Herbert M., and Arthur J. Levin. "The Housing Assistance Plan: A Non-Working Program for Community Improvement." Washington, D.C.: The Potomac Institute, Inc., November 1975.

Frieden, Bernard J., and Marshall Kaplan. Community Development and the Model Cities Legacy. Cambridge, Mass.: Joint Center for Urban Studies of MIT and Harvard University, November 1976.

Ginsberg, Robert L., Mary K. Nenno, and Deena R. Sosson. NAHRO: Year 1 Findings—Community Development Block Grants. Washington, D.C.: National Association of Housing and Redevelopment Officials, April 1976.

Ginsberg, Robert L. "Second Year Community Development Block Grant Experience: A Summary of Findings of the NAHRO Community Development Project." Journal of Housing 34 (February 1977): 80-83.

LeGates, Richard T., and Mary C. Morgan. "The Perils of Special Revenue Sharing for Community Development." Journal of the American Institute of Planners 39 (July 1973): 254-64.

Liebschutz, Sarah F. "Community Development Block Grants: Who Benefits?" Paper prepared for delivery at the 1977 Annual Meeting of the American Political Science Association, Washington, D.C., September 1-4, 1977.

Michigan Advisory Committee to the U.S. Commission on Civil Rights. Civil Rights and the Housing and Community Development Act of 1974. Volume 1: Livonia. Washington, D.C.: U.S. Government Printing Office, June 1975.

_____. Volume II: A Comparison with Model Cities. Washington, D.C.: U.S. Government Printing Office, June 1976.

_____. Volume III: The Chippewa People of Sault Ste. Marie. Washington, D.C.: U.S. Government Printing Office, November 1976.

Nathan, Richard P., Paul R. Dommel, Sarah F. Liebschutz, Milton D. Morris, and associates. Block Grants for Community Development. Washington, D.C.: U.S. Department of Housing and Community Development, January 1977.

_____. "Monitoring the Block Grant Program for Community Development." Political Science Quarterly 92 (Summer 1977): 219-44.

National Urban League. The New Housing Programs: Who Benefits? New York: National Urban League, 1975.

Nenno, Mary K. "Second Year Community Development Experience." Journal of Housing 34 (April 1977): 182-85.

Southern California Association of Governments. SCAG Review of Second Year Housing and Community Development Title I Block Grant Applications. Los Angeles: Southern California Association of Governments, November 1976.

U.S. Advisory Commission on Intergovernmental Relations. Community Development: The Workings of a Federal-Local Block Grant. Washington, D.C.: March 1977.

U.S. Commission on Federal Paperwork. Housing Programs. Washington, D.C.: June 10, 1977.

U.S. Congress. House. Committee on Banking, Finance and Urban Affairs. Subcommittee on Housing and Community Development. Community Development Block Grant Program. Committee Print. 95th Cong., 1st sess., 1977.

U.S. Congress. House. Committee on Banking and Currency. Subcommittee on Housing. Compilation of the Housing and Community Development Act of 1974. Committee Print. 93rd Cong., 2d sess., 1974.

U.S. Congress. House. Committee on Banking, Currency and Housing. Subcommittee on Housing and Community Development. Evolution of Role of the Federal Government in Housing and Community Development: A Chronology of Selected Executive Actions, 1892-1974. Committee Print. 94th Cong., 1st sess., 1975.

U.S. Council on Environmental Quality. "Community Development Block Grants and NEPA: Delegation of National Environmental Policy Act Responsibilities to Community Development Block Grant Recipients." Washington, D.C.: U.S. Council on Environmental Quality, May 1977.

U.S. Department of Housing and Urban Development. A-95 Project Notification and Review System: An Evaluation Related to Community Development Block Grants. Washington, D.C.: U.S. Government Printing Office, November 1976.

_____. Community Development Block Grant Entitlement Cities: The First Year Planning and Application Process. Washington, D.C.: U.S. Government Printing Office, August 1976.

_____. Community Development Block Grant Program: First Annual Report. Washington, D.C.: U.S. Government Printing Office, December 1975.

_____. Community Development Block Grant Program: Second Annual Report. Washington, D.C.: U.S. Government Printing Office, December 1976.

_____. Community Development Block Grant Program: Third Annual Report. Washington, D.C.: U.S. Government Printing Office, March 1978.

U.S. General Accounting Office. Environmental Reviews Done by Communities: Are They Needed? Are They Adequate? September 1, 1977.

_____. Management and Evaluation of the Community Development Block Grant Program Need to Be Strengthened. August 30, 1978.

_____. Meeting Application and Review Requirements for Block Grants under Title I of the Housing and Community Development Act of 1974. June 23, 1976.

_____. Why the Formula for Allocating Community Development Block Grants Should Be Improved. December 6, 1976.

Witte, William. "Community Development's Third Year: A Report on Trends and Findings of NAHRO's CD Monitoring Project." Journal of Housing 35 (February 1978): 66-72.

The Intergovernmental System

Beer, Samuel H. "The Adoption of General Revenue Sharing: A Case Study in Public Sector Politics." Public Policy 24 (Spring 1976): 127-95.

Break, George F. Intergovernmental Fiscal Relations in the United States. Washington, D.C.: Brookings, 1967.

Bryce, James. The American Commonwealth. 3 vols. London: Macmillan, 1888.

Burgess, John W. "The American Commonwealth." Political Science Quarterly 1 (March 1886): 9-35.

Carey, Jane Perry Clark. The Rise of a New Federalism. New York: Columbia University Press, 1938.

Demuth, Christopher C. "Deregulating the Cities." The Public Interest no. 44 (1976): 115-28.

Derthick, Martha. The Influence of Federal Grants: Public Assistance in Massachusetts. Cambridge, Mass.: Harvard University Press, 1970.

_____. New Towns In-Town. Washington, D.C.: The Urban Institute, 1972.

Frieden, Bernard J., and Marshall Kaplan. The Politics of Neglect: Urban Aid from Model Cities to Revenue Sharing. Cambridge, Mass.: MIT Press, 1975.

Hansen, Alvin J., and Harvey S. Perloff. State and Local Finance in the National Economy. New York: W. W. Norton, 1944.

Heller, Walter W. New Dimensions of Political Economy. New York: W. W. Norton, 1967.

Inman, Robert P., Martin McGuire, Wallace E. Oates, Jeffrey L. Pressman, and Robert D. Reischauer. Financing the New Federalism. Baltimore: Johns Hopkins University Press, 1975.

Key, V. O. The Administration of Federal Grants to the States. Chicago: Public Administration Service, 1937.

Moynihan, Daniel P. Maximum Feasible Misunderstanding. New York: Free Press, 1970.

Nathan, Richard P. The Plot That Failed: Nixon and the Administrative Presidency. New York: Wiley, 1975.

Nathan, Richard P., Allen D. Manvel, Susannah E. Calkins, and associates. Monitoring Revenue Sharing. Washington, D.C.: Brookings, 1975.

Nathan, Richard P., Charles F. Adams, Jr., and associates. Revenue Sharing: The Second Round. Washington, D.C.: Brookings, 1977.

Oates, Wallace E., ed. The Political Economy of Fiscal Federalism. Lexington, Mass.: Lexington Books, 1977.

Patten, Simon N. "Decay of State and Local Government." Annals of the American Academy of Political and Social Science 1 (July 1890): 26–42.

Pressman, Jeffrey L. Federal Programs and City Politics: The Dynamics of the Aid Process in Oakland. Berkeley: University of California Press, 1975.

Reuss, Henry S. Revenue Sharing: Crutch or Catalyst for State and Local Governments? New York: Praeger, 1970.

Sneed, Joseph D., and Steven A. Waldhorn, eds. Restructuring the Federal System: Approaches to Accountability in Postcategorical Programs. New York: Crane, Russak, 1975.

Stenberg, Carl W. "Block Grants in Transition: The Politics of Decategorization and Recategorization." Paper prepared for delivery at the 1977 Annual Meeting of the American Political Science Association, Washington, D.C., September 1–4, 1977.

Sundquist, James L., with David W. Davis. Making Federalism Work: A Study of Program Coordination at the Community Level. Washington, D.C.: Brookings, 1969.

Thompson, Walter. Federal Centralization. New York: Harcourt, Brace, 1923.

U.S. Advisory Commission on Intergovernmental Relations. Block Grants: A Comparative Analysis. Washington, D.C.: U.S. Government Printing Office, October 1977.

_____. Categorical Grants: Their Role and Design. Washington, D.C.: U.S. Government Printing Office, May 1978.

_____. A Catalog of Federal Grant-in-Aid Programs to State and Local Governments: Grants Funded FY 1975. Washington, D.C.: U.S. Government Printing Office, October 1977.

_____. A Catalog of Federal Grant-in-Aid Programs to State and Local Governments: Grants Funded FY 1978. Washington, D.C.: U.S. Government Printing Office, February 1979.

_____. The Comprehensive Employment and Training Act: Early Readings for a Hybrid Block Grant. Washington, D.C.: U.S. Government Printing Office, June 1977.

_____. Improving Federal Grants Management. Washington, D.C.: U.S. Government Printing Office, February 1977.

_____. The Intergovernmental Grant System as Seen by Local, State, and Federal Officials. Washington, D.C.: U.S. Government Printing Office, March 1977.

_____. The Partnership for Health Act: Lessons from a Pioneering Block Grant. Washington, D.C.: U.S. Government Printing Office, January 1977.

_____. Safe Streets Reconsidered: The Block Grant Experience 1968-1975. Washington, D.C.: U.S. Government Printing Office, January 1977.

_____. Summary and Concluding Observations. Washington, D.C.: U.S. Government Printing Office, June 1978.

U.S. Commission on Intergovernmental Relations (Kestnbaum Commission). A Report to the President for Transmittal to Congress. Washington, D.C.: U.S. Government Printing Office, June 1955.

U.S. Congressional Budget Office. Federal Constraints on State and Local Government Actions. Washington, D.C.: U.S. Government Printing Office, April 1979.

U.S. Executive Office of the President, Study Committee on Policy Management Assistance. Strengthening Public Management in the Intergovernmental System. Washington, D.C.: U.S. Government Printing Office, 1975.

U.S. General Accounting Office. Fundamental Changes Are Needed in Federal Assistance to State and Local Governments. August 19, 1975.

U.S. National Commission on Urban Problems. Building the American City. Washington, D.C.: U.S. Government Printing Office, 1968.

Wilson, James Q., ed. Urban Renewal: The Record and the Controversy. Cambridge, Mass.: MIT Press, 1966.

Local Government

Banfield, Edward C. Political Influence: A New Theory of Urban Politics. New York: Free Press, 1961.

_____. The Unheavenly City Revisited. Boston: Little, Brown, 1974.

Banfield, Edward C., and James Q. Wilson. City Politics. New York: Vintage, 1963.

Dahl, Robert A. Who Governs? Democracy and Power in an American City. New Haven: Yale University Press, 1961.

Downs, Anthony. Opening Up the Suburbs. New Haven: Yale University Press, 1973.

Hawley, Willis D., and David Rogers, eds. Improving the Quality of Urban Management. Beverly Hills: Sage Publications, 1974.

Levy, Frank, Arnold J. Meltsner, and Aaron Wildavsky. Urban Outcomes: Schools, Streets, and Libraries. Berkeley: University of California Press, 1974.

Long, Norton E. The Unwalled City: Reconstituting the Urban Community. New York: Basic Books, 1972.

Lowe, Jeanne R. Cities in a Race with Time. New York: Vintage, 1967.

Meyerson, Martin, and Edward C. Banfield. Politics, Planning, and the Public Interest. New York: Free Press, 1955.

Powledge, Fred. Model City. New York: Simon and Schuster, 1970.

Pressman, Jeffrey L. "Preconditions of Mayoral Leadership." American Political Science Review 66 (June 1972): 511-24.

Selby, Earl. "New Haven: Where Federal Dollars Pay Off." Reader's Digest 94 (June 1969): 189-96.

Talbot, Allan R. The Mayor's Game: Richard Lee of New Haven and the Politics of Change. New York: Praeger, 1970.

Wolfinger, Raymond E. The Politics of Progress. Englewood Cliffs, N.J.: Prentice-Hall, 1974.

Yates, Douglas. "The Federal Government and the Urban Crisis." New York Affairs 3 (1976): 28-41.

_____. The Ungovernable City: The Politics of Urban Problems and Policy Making. Cambridge, Mass.: MIT Press, 1977).

Bureaucratic Behavior

Allison, Graham T. Essence of Decision: Explaining the Cuban Missile Crisis. Boston: Little, Brown, 1971.

Downs, Anthony. Inside Bureaucracy. Boston: Little, Brown, 1967.

Heclo, Hugh. A Government of Strangers: Executive Politics in Washington. Washington, D.C.: Brookings, 1977.

Holden, Jr., Matthew. "'Imperialism' in Bureaucracy." American Political Science Review 60 (December 1966): 943-51.

Kaufman, Herbert. "Emerging Conflicts in the Doctrines of Public Administration." American Political Science Review 50 (December 1956): 1057-73.

_____. The Limits of Organizational Change. University: University of Alabama Press, 1971.

_____. Red Tape: Its Origins, Uses, and Abuses. Washington, D.C.: Brookings, 1977.

Rourke, Francis E. Bureaucracy, Politics, and Public Policy. Boston: Little, Brown, 1976.

Seidman, Harold. Politics, Position, and Power: The Dynamics of Federal Organization. New York: Oxford University Press, 1975.

Budgeting and Implementation

Bailey, Stephen K., and Edith K. Mosher. ESEA: The Office of Education Administers a Law. Syracuse, N.Y.: Syracuse University Press, 1968.

Bardach, Eugene. The Implementation Game: What Happens After a Bill Becomes a Law. Cambridge, Mass.: MIT Press, 1977.

Bardach, Eugene, and Lucian Pugliaresi. "The Environmental Impact Statement vs. the Real World." The Public Interest no. 49 (Fall 1977): 22-38.

Levine, Robert A. Public Planning: Failure and Redirection. New York: Basic Books, 1972.

Lindblom, Charles E. The Intelligence of Democracy. New York: Free Press, 1965.

Lowi, Theodore J. "American Business, Public Policy, Case-Studies, and Political Theory." World Politics 16 (July 1974): 677-715.

_____. The End of Liberalism: Ideology, Policy, and the Crisis of Public Authority. New York: W. W. Norton, 1969.

Murphy, Jerome T. State Education Agencies and Discretionary Funds. Lexington, Mass.: Lexington Books, 1974.

_____. "Title I of ESEA: The Politics of Implementing Federal Educational Reform." Harvard Educational Review 41 (February 1971): 35-63.

Pressman, Jeffrey L., and Aaron B. Wildavsky. Implementation. Berkeley: University of California Press, 1973.

Wildavsky, Aaron. The Politics of the Budgetary Process. Boston: Little, Brown, 1974.

Williams, Walter, and Richard F. Elmore, eds. Social Program Implementation. New York: Academic Press, 1976.

INDEX

ABOUT THE AUTHOR

DONALD F. KETTL is Assistant Professor of Government and Foreign Affairs at the University of Virginia. He was previously Assistant Professor of Political Science at Columbia University.

Professor Kettl's main interests are in the areas of intergovernmental relations, policy analysis, and public management. He has published an earlier article on community development in <u>Political Science Quarterly</u> and a series of management cases with the Intercollegiate Case Clearing House.

<u>Managing Community Development in the New Federalism</u> was the recipient of the American Political Science Association William Anderson Award for the best doctoral dissertation in 1978 in the field of intergovernmental relations in the United States.

Professor Kettl holds B.A., M.A., M.Phil., and Ph.D. degrees from Yale University.